"Giving people choices in health care and instilling cost-consciousness is plain old common sense. In Medical Savings Accounts, authors Goodman and Musgrave have hit upon a bold concept that may revolutionize the way health care is delivered throughout America."

—Sen. Phil Gramm

Sponsor of a bill in Congress to implement Medical Savings Accounts, the clearest alternative to government-run health care

PATIENT POWER

The Free-Enterprise Alternative to Clinton's Health Plan

John C. Goodman and Gerald L. Musgrave

CATO INSTITUTE

This is an abridged version of *Patient Power: Solving America's Health Care Crisis* by John C. Goodman and Gerald L. Musgrave (Washington: Cato Institute, 1992). This abridgment was prepared by Michael D. Tanner, director of health and welfare studies at the Cato Institute.

ISBN: 1-882577-10-8

Printed in the United States of America.

Cato Institute
1000 Massachusetts Avenue, N.W.
Washington, D.C. 20001

Contents

Preface

A thorough economic analysis of the health care system in the United States is complex, not because special theories are needed, but because health care is the most regulated and most politicized sector of our economy. It takes considerable understanding of economics, medical care, politics, ethics, and emotions before anyone can obtain a unified view of health care. Our book, *Patient Power,* is a synthesis of those aspects. This abridged volume is a condensation of that synthesis.

The thesis of this book is simple: if we want to solve the nation's health care crisis, we must apply the same common-sense principles to medical care that we apply to other goods and services.

In a 1991 *New York Times*/CBS News poll, almost 80 percent of the respondents agreed that the American "health care system is headed toward a crisis because of rising costs."[1] The irony is that health care costs are rising because, for individual patients, medical care is cheap, not expensive.

On the average, patients pay only 5 cents out-of-pocket for every dollar they spend in hospitals. The remainder is paid by private and public health insurance. Patients pay less than 19 cents out-of-pocket for every dollar they spend on physicians' services, and they pay less than 24 cents of every dollar they spend on health care of all types. Patients therefore have an incentive to purchase hospital services until, at the margin, they're worth only 5 cents on the dollar and to purchase physicians' services until they are worth only 19 cents on the dollar. The wonder is that we don't spend even more than we do.

Health care is often said to be a necessity. However, there

---

[1] Erick Eckholm, "Health Benefits Found to Deter Job Switching," *New York Times,* September 26, 1991.

are other necessities such as food, clothing, housing, and transportation. If we paid for any of those items the way we pay for health care, we would face a similar crisis. If we paid only 5 cents on the dollar for food, clothing, or housing, for example, costs would explode in each of those markets.[2]

If we are to control health care costs, we must be prepared to make tough decisions about how much to spend on medical care versus other goods and services. So far, we have avoided such choices, confident that health care spending can be determined by "needs," rather than by choices among competing alternatives. In that respect, the U.S. health care system is unique. The United States is the only country in the world where people can consume medical care almost without limit, unconstrained by marketprices or by government rationing.

Consider the case of an 80-year-old man who suffered from the condition of "slowing down." Despite the physician's counsel that the condition was perfectly normal at age 80, the patient and his wife went on a literal shopping spree in the medical marketplace. As the physician explained to the *New York Times:*

> A few days ago the couple came in for a follow-up visit. They were upset. At their daughter's insistence they had gone to an out-of-town neurologist. She had wanted the "best" for her father and would spare no (Medicare) expense to get it. The patient had undergone a CAT scan, a magnetic resonance imaging, a spinal tap, a brain-stem evoke potential and a carotid duplex ultrasound.
>
> No remediable problems were discovered. The Medicare billing was more than $4,000 so far . . . but they were emotionally exhausted by the experience and anxious over what portion of the

---

[2] For a tongue-in-cheek, but perfectly accurate, analysis of the consequences of treating nutrition as we do medicine, see Gerald L. Musgrave, Leigh Tripoli, and Fu Ling Yu, "Lunch Insurance," *Regulation* 15, no. 4 (Fall 1992): 16-24.

expenses might not be covered by insurance.

I have seen this Medicare madness happen too often. It is caused by many factors, but contrary to public opinion, physician greed is not high on the list. I tried to stop the crime, but found I was just a pawn in a ruthless game, whose rules are excess and waste. Who will stop the madness?[3]

The potential demand for health care is virtually unlimited. Even if there were a limit to what medical science can do (which, over time, there isn't), there is an almost endless list of ailments that can motivate our desire to spend. About 83 million people suffer from insomnia, 70 million have severe headaches, 32 million have arthritis, 23 million have allergies, and 16 million have bad backs. Even when the illnesses are not real, our minds have incredible power to convince us that they are.

If the only way to control health care costs is to have someone choose between health care and money (that is, other goods and services), who should that someone be? There are only two fundamental alternatives: the choices must be made either by the patients themselves or by a health care bureaucracy that is ultimately answerable to government. This book makes the case for the patients.

Almost all arguments against empowering patients are variations on the notion that individuals are not smart enough or knowledgeable enough to make wise decisions. But if that argument is persuasive in health care, why isn't it equally persuasive in every other area of life? With respect to almost any decision we make, someone else is always smarter or more knowledgeable than we are. If the case for freedom rested on the assumption that free individuals always make perfect decisions, we would have discarded liberty and democracy long ago.

The case for empowering patients rests on a different

---

[3] Elliot Rosenberg, letter to the editor, *New York Times,* September 18, 1991.

assumption. No one cares more about us than we do. Thus, while prudent people seek and get advice from specialists before making many decisions, it does not follow that we should turn control of our lives over to the experts. In the long run, more good than bad decisions are made when self-interested individuals are free to accept or reject advice from many quarters.

A corollary to the goal of empowering patients is the goal of creating competitive markets in the health care sector, for physicians' services, hospital services, health insurance, and other services. Individuals pursuing their own interests in a market are best served by suppliers who compete vigorously to meet consumer needs with high-quality services produced at the lowest possible cost.

This book represents a radical departure from the conventional wisdom in the field of health policy. Whereas the vast majority of health policy commentators take a bureaucratic approach to health care, our approach is individualistic, focusing on the decisions that individuals make and the incentives they face when they make them. Whereas the vast majority of health policy proposals call for more regulation and more government spending, we find that government is the problem, not the solution—that solving America's health care crisis requires undoing the harmful distortions introduced into the system by government and that only a market-based system will work.

The dominant view of health policy is regularly reported in the national news media and parroted by syndicated columnists, editorial writers, and politicians. What is needed in health care, they tell us, is not competition but monopoly. Instead of empowering individuals, they assert, we should empower the bureaucracy. Rather than look to the private sector for solutions, we should look to government. When speaking to the general public, the socialism-works-in-health-care crowd points to national health insurance in other countries, arguing that the quality is high, the cost is low, and the vast majority of people like it. Behind closed doors, though, they tell politicians that other countries control health care costs by refusing to spend money and by forcing doctors to ration health care.

It is no surprise that most people who live under national health insurance like it. For minor aches and pains, they have no difficulty seeing general practitioners and they perceive such services to be "free." But that's not a useful test of a health care system. In any given year, only about 4 percent of the population requires access to the remarkable advances made possible by modern medical science. The better test is: When people need such services, can they get them? And if they do get them, how long do they have to wait? It is in answering those questions that we uncover the worst tragedies of socialized medicine.

The case of Joel Bondy illustrates what we could be facing. Joel was a two-year-old child with a serious congenital heart defect that urgently needed surgery. It was a serious operation, but one that was performed many times in hospitals across the United States. Unfortunately, Joel did not live in this country. He lived in Canada, where the country's national health care system has resulted in a severe shortage of cardiac care facilities. In fact, Canada has only 11 open-heart surgery facilities to serve the entire country, compared to 793 in the United States.

Joel's operation was repeatedly postponed as more critical cases preempted the available facilities. Alarmed at their son's deteriorating condition, Joel's parents arranged for him to be operated on in Detroit. When word of this case reached the Canadian media, embarrassed authorities told the Bondys that, if they would stay in Canada, Joel would be moved to the top of the waiting list and could have his surgery immediately. Joel was taken on a four-hour ambulance ride to the nearest hospital equipped for the procedure, but there was no bed available. The family had to spend the night in a hotel. Joel Bondy died the next day without ever reaching surgery.[4]

---

[4] John A. Barnes, "Canadians Cross Border to Save Their Lives," *Wall Street Journal,* December 12, 1990.

Such a tragedy could easily become commonplace in this country if we make the wrong decisions on how to reform our health care system.

No one doubts that the American medical marketplace today is badly in need of reform. In a normal market, producers search for ways to satisfy consumer needs for a price consumers are willing to pay. Demand is a given. The problem for producers is to reduce the costs of meeting that demand. However, in the American health care system, the opposite is true. All too often, consumer preferences are regarded as irrelevant. Producers decide what their costs are going to be and then wrestle with getting consumers to pay those costs— through out-of-pocket payments, through employers and insurance companies, or through the government.

In a normal market, increases in sales are universally regarded as good. The more consumers buy, the more their needs are being met. If domestic automobile sales increased each year as a percentage of our gross national product, most people would cheer. In health care the opposite is true. The annual increase in health care services is viewed not as a benefit but as a burden.

In the topsy-turvy world of health care, what would normally be viewed as "good" is considered "bad," and vice versa. Thus, to truly understand the medical marketplace, we have to discover all of the ways in which normal market forces have been undermined.

In this book we use the term "cost-plus finance" to describe the predominant way in which we are currently paying for medical services. In contrast, we propose a health care system that we call Patient Power, a system that is based on empowering individual patients and the strength of competitive markets.

Key to the Patient Power system are medical savings accounts. Medical savings accounts are tax-deferred accounts set up to pay for routine medical care and to allow for savings to pay future medical expenses. Medical savings accounts would allow employers, self-employed individuals, and others to purchase a high-deductible health insurance policy and put the premium savings into a medical savings account to pay for routine medical care. The funds in the medical savings account would belong to the individual, and if not spent, would accumulate over time as savings to be used for future health care expenses.

Medical savings accounts put the patient back in charge of health care, making him a buyer as well as a user of care. The result will be a reduction in health care costs, reduced administrative overhead, a strengthening of the patient-physician relationship, and greater access to care for those now lacking health insurance.

1.
America's Health Care Crisis

America's health care system is in crisis. That's the conclusion of virtually every commentator on American medicine, regardless of political persuasion. Ask any doctor, any patient, any business executive or politician. Indeed, virtually everyone who has even remote contact with health care agrees that the system is in serious need of reform.

The crisis is not new. It has been emerging for at least two decades. Over that period, an almost unlimited number of recommendations for reform have been made. Yet we are no closer to solving the crisis today than we were 20 years ago.

One reason there is no consensus on the solution is that there is no agreement on the problem. What each of us believes the nature of the crisis to be depends on where we stand in relation to the health care system.

Why We Can't Agree on the Nature of the Crisis

For employers and many public officials, the crisis is one of costs. America, they remind us, is spending more than $800 billion a year on health care—about $3,200 per year for every man, woman, and child. Health care spending exceeds 14 percent of our gross national product, more than in any other country in the world.

Yet for every cry of alarm over rising health care spending, there are at least two or three cries over our failure to spend more. Some 37 million Americans, we are told, lack health insurance. The policies of many who do have health insurance exclude mental health care or treatment for alcohol and drug abuse. Then there is a seemingly endless list of unmet health care needs: prenatal care for the young, nursing home care for the old, organ transplants, and underfunded medical research. The most popular measures before Congress and the state legislatures are proposals not to lower health care spending but to extend health insurance to more people and more services.

The conflict of perspectives does not end there. For example, to most doctors, the main problem is bureaucratic interference from government, insurers, employers, and even hospital administrators—interference that raises costs and sometimes lowers the quality of patient care. But to almost all third-party (insurance) payers and many hospital administrators, the problem is that doctors have too much freedom—especially to increase prices. Almost every patient who sees a hospital bill believes the hospital overcharges. Almost all employers and insurance companies share that view. But almost all hospital administrators believe their hospitals are undercompensated and worry about what services they will cut if they do not somehow increase revenues.

Before examining those conflicting perspectives, it is worthwhile to consider how they develop.

A Trip through the Health Care System with the Wilson Family

The people in the following vignettes are fictitious. The kinds of events described are real, however, and occur all too frequently.

Jeff Wilson (Patient)

Jeff Wilson was furious. He had been out of the hospital for more than a month, but "$3,296.24" was indelibly stamped in his mind. That was the bill for minor surgery and a few days' stay in a hospital run by his own brother! He tried to see the other side of things. That was what his wife,

June, kept telling him to do. Sure, hospital costs were up—hospitals could do a lot more things these days. And his share of the bill was less than $800. Blue Cross would pay the rest, or at least that was what he initially thought. Still, it was the principle of the thing.

He had gone to see his brother about the bill. "Bob," he had said, "there's got to be some mistake here. Fifteen dollars for one Tylenol tablet? You've got to be kidding. Had I known that, I would have gotten out of my sickbed, walked across the street, and bought my own Tylenol." It was Bob's attitude that bothered him more than anything else. Bob wouldn't even back down on the price of the hospital admission kit, which had contained personal items such as a toothbrush, comb, and small razor. "Twenty-five dollars for a little kit, just like the ones airlines give you for free on international flights? C'mon, Bob, that's ridiculous," he had said.

"Maybe it would have ended there, with me blowing off some steam," Jeff thought. "But hell, I'm a businessman. I see these damn insurance premiums going up year after year, and no wonder—$15 for a Tylenol tablet?" That's why he'd gone to Blue Cross. He'd felt a little guilty, pointing a big insurance company toward his brother. Still, Blue Cross was paying 80 percent of the bill. And somebody has to do something about health care costs, don't they?

Things hadn't worked out in quite the way he'd expected. Oh, they had been pleasant enough at Blue Cross. The woman had listened carefully. She'd promised to look into the matter. But somehow Jeff had known at the time that nothing was going to change.

He'd almost gotten over the whole thing. Until last night when June had invited Bob over for dinner. It was supposed to be the time for reconciliation. "And I certainly tried to be nice," Jeff thought. The trouble had started when Bob made that comment about the hospital's charges.

"Look at it this way, Jeff," Bob had said. "You paid less than $800 for three days in the hospital. That's about what you'd pay to stay in a nice hotel without any medical care at all. That's cheap."

"Sure, that made me angry," Jeff thought. "But I controlled it. Without even raising my voice, I patiently explained to Bob how health insurance premiums work. June was probably right. I probably was patronizing. Maybe that's why Bob got personal."

"Jeff, you and I both know that you took advantage of your health insurance, just like everybody else does," Bob had said. "Your doctor told you that the surgery could be done as an outpatient. But you both agreed you'd check into the hospital and rest for a couple of days because your health insurance would pick up most of the tab. You and June thought that was a great idea."

That had made him even angrier, Jeff remembered. But he'd controlled himself. In fact, he'd controlled his emotions all evening—until Bob brought up that stuff about Blue Cross.

Bob Wilson (Jeff's Brother, Hospital Administrator)

Bob Wilson was feeling unsettled. He never should have told Jeff about the deal with Blue Cross. He'd known it was a mistake the minute he'd said it. "Jeff," he'd said, "we have a special deal with Blue Cross. They paid a flat rate of $640 for each day you were in the hospital. They couldn't care less what was on your hospital bill." That was when Jeff hit the roof.

"No question. That was a mistake. But the biggest mistake is what the hospital's computers keep putting on patients' statements," Bob thought. Jeff's hospital statement stretched halfway across Bob's office. Jeff could probably read only four words on the whole thing—"Tylenol tablet" and "admission kit." But Jeff had found them. That's the way Jeff was.

What had they said at the hospital convention last year? "Take the line items that patients can recognize and can buy on their own. Next to those items put 'no charge' and make up the difference by raising some other price that they don't understand. Make the patients think they're getting a good deal. That way, they're happy. You're happy. Everybody's happy." "Brilliant," Bob had thought at the time. He just hadn't gotten around to it. There were so many problems. Like Mr. Hansen.

Hansen had come to the emergency room the previous Saturday. Seventy years old. Dying of prostate cancer. Unable to take oral medication. Family did not know how to give injectables. "So what do you do? You admit him to the hospital," Bob thought. "At least that's what we would have done 10 years ago. But not today. Medicare won't pay." "Acute care not justified" is the official bureaucratese for the whole thing.

"Not justified," Bob thought. The next day, Hansen was dead. Bob felt irritated without understanding why. Hansen wasn't the first case like that. Why did it bother him so much? Maybe it was that scene with the emergency room physician on Monday morning. "Your hospital rules are killing people, and I'm resigning as of now," the physician had said. Bob could identify with that. He'd probably have done the same thing 30 years ago.

"But what can you do?" Bob said out loud. "Medicaid pays 50 cents on the dollar, Medicare won't pay to save a patient's life, and Jeff complains because he's been charged a few extra dollars for a stupid pill!"

"Only a few more years until retirement," Bob thought, as he became more reflective. Too many tragedies . . . like June's mother. He could never tell Jeff and June about what really happened there. No . . . he'd take that one to his grave.

Kay Pierce (June Wilson's Physician)

Kay Pierce was unhappy. Why had she ever gone into medicine in the first place, she wondered. "You get to help people and you get paid a lot of money for doing it." That's what they'd told her when she'd entered medical school. But they hadn't told her the rest of the story.

June Wilson had just been to see Kay about her tension

headaches. That's what Kay thought they were. Still, there was always some chance. . . . When Kay had talked about expensive tests, June wasn't interested. But when Kay told her that she could fill out the forms so that Blue Cross would pay for most of it, June's attitude changed.

"So here we are," Kay thought, "about $3,000 later, including the magnetic resonance imaging (MRI) scan, hospital admission (so Blue Cross would pay), physician visits, and prescription drugs—lots of drugs. People want to know why health care is so expensive? I think I'll write an article and explain it," she thought. "Let's see, if half the people in the country have tension headaches and if we spend $3,000 on each of them. . . . " Kay was confident that was going to be a very large number. But as she reached for her calculator, another thought struck her. There were also cases like June's mother.

June's mother, Irene, had been Kay's patient, too. Formerly a heavy smoker, Irene should have gotten a chest x-ray each year. But there was the problem with Medicare. Irene didn't show any symptoms of cancer (no coughing, for example), and Medicare won't pay for screening tests if there are no symptoms. On the other hand, if Irene had paid for the x-ray with her own money, there would have been other problems. Kay would have had to complete a complicated form and spend at least 20 minutes explaining to Irene why Medicare wouldn't pay. That's time for which she couldn't bill Irene.

Kay could have lied to Medicare by writing a symptom such as "coughing" on the Medicare reimbursement form. She'd done that before. But it was risky. She could have given Irene a free x-ray. But if she provided free screening tests for all of her Medicare patients, she'd go broke. Besides, Irene had seemed so healthy.

Irene did have lung cancer, and by the time Kay discovered it, it was too late—six months later she was dead. "It was the most traumatic thing I've ever been through," Kay thought. Talking to her friend Jack, an oncologist, helped a lot. "Kay, it's not your fault," Jack had said. "In my field, Medicare kills people all the time. The government won't pay for the best drugs, so we treat cancer patients with inferior drugs. If I took personal responsibility for every preventable death, I'd have to check into a mental institution."

"People need to know about these things," Kay had told Jack.

"Yeah, but unless you want a malpractice suit, you're not the one to tell them," Jack had said. Kay thought about that. Then she remembered another problem she'd heard about at the hospital that day—the problem involving Jeff Wilson's father.

Mark Wilson (Jeff's Cousin, Pacemaker Manufacturer)

Mark Wilson was angry. What had he spent his whole adult life doing? Nothing less than making the best pacemakers in the whole world. And what did his cousin, Jeff, do when his own father needed a pacemaker? Totally ignored every damn thing he told him!

The incident began over a year ago, when Jeff's father George was diagnosed as having a heart problem. But Mark found out just this morning what had ultimately happened. He vividly remembered his conversation with Jeff when the issue first came up. "Jeff," he had said, "I make pacemakers. Now I can sell you an old-fashioned one, or I can sell you a really good one. The government won't pay for the good ones. But your father's still employed. That means he's covered by private insurance, not by Medicare. I'll tell you what kind of pacemaker to get, and you make sure George gets it."

Mark had assumed it had all been taken care of. Until this morning, that is. Mark was talking to George on the phone when he casually asked what kind of pacemaker George had. It was the wrong kind. Not wanting to alarm George, he controlled his anger and got off the phone as quickly as possible. He showed no such restraint when he got George's doctor on the phone. Before the doctor could hang up on him, Mark learned that George's private insurance carrier had adopted the same policy as Medicare. They refused to pay for higher quality pacemakers.

Mark had always thought that government was the greatest single threat to Western civilization. But it was increasingly clear to him that insurance companies were in second place and closing fast. The only thought that comforted him was his decision to end his company's employee health insurance plan. "What more evidence," he thought, "does anyone need to see the correctness of that decision?"

About three months earlier, Mark had met with his accountant. "We're a small company competing with Williams, Inc., a giant multinational," Mark had said. "The only way we can compete is to keep our costs down. So let's make sure our health insurance costs are below theirs."

"Can't be done, Mark," his accountant had said. "Why not?" Mark had asked. "Because Williams has a no-frills, bare-bones policy. Your policy covers acupuncture, in vitro fertilization, alcohol and drug abuse treatment, chiropractic services, and lots of other extras."

"Then get rid of the frills," said Mark, without thinking twice about it. "Can't," said the accountant. "Why not?" asked Mark. "State law," the accountant said. "Well, how the hell does Williams get around all that?" asked Mark. "Williams is a large company," he was told. "Federal law allows large companies to escape state regulation. Small companies can't escape."

That's when Mark decided he'd had it with health insurance. For the past two years his company had faced premium increases of 30 percent per year. "At that rate, we'll be bankrupt in five years," Mark had told his employees. To compensate, Mark gave every employee a $750 bonus to buy their own health insurance if they wanted it.

"But Mark," his accountant had said, "you've got to take taxes out of that $750. And lots of employees will just spend the remainder on other things. You're going to have a lot of people around here without any health insurance."

Privately, that thought bothered Mark. But it bothered him even more that Williams, Inc., had a way out of this problem, and he didn't. "There's government again," he thought, "sticking it to the little guy. And what am I supposed to do about it? It's better for the employees to be without health insurance than without jobs."

Then Mark remembered that his sister worked for a U.S. senator who was very involved in health care issues. He decided to give her a call.

Nancy Wilson (Mark's Sister, Aide to a U.S. Senator)

Nancy Wilson was troubled. She had just talked by phone with her brother Mark. What Mark had said bothered her. But what bothered her even more was the conversation she'd had with Senator Blake the day before.

She'd worked for the senator for two years. Since Blake was the most important person in Congress on health care issues, she'd received many telephone calls in those two years from people all over the country—people just like Mark, but with far more serious problems. In most cases, the senator gave her brief instructions on how to handle the problem (send a letter to this person, place a call to that person). But yesterday the senator had really talked with her.

He had just come back from an important meeting. "Nancy," he'd said, "let me tell you how health care works in this country. If we did everything doctors know how to do to help people, we would spend our entire gross national product on health care. Nobody but a lunatic would suggest that. So what we do is say to the medical community, 'This is all the money you get; you figure out how to spend it.'"

"We don't put any restrictions on how they spend it?" Nancy had asked.

"Restrictions?" Blake had responded. "Of course we've got restrictions. Thousands of them. Medical care in this country is an $800-billion-a-year industry and every interest group is here in Washington trying to get a slice of it. We've got so many special-interest rules that I don't know how the hospitals keep track of them."

"Nancy, we can pass laws all day and all night, and it's not going to matter whether the hospitals obey them or break them. The bottom line is this. If you don't have money, you can't give care. The squeeze is on. And if the hospitals think they're being squeezed now, they have no idea how bad it's going to get."

"But why can't you just explain to people what the problems are?" Nancy had asked.

"Because nobody dares," Blake had retorted. "You can't talk authoritatively about something unless you know about it. You can't know about it unless you've participated in the decisions. And if you've been involved in the decisions, then you're personally responsible for causing people a lot of harm. If I admitted what I do here in Washington, I'd never get reelected."

"But what do people in other countries do?" Nancy had asked.

"It's worse. In Britain, doctors probably spend more time denying people care than giving it."

Nancy had been baffled. The problems were worse than she had ever imagined. "So what can we do?" she had blurted.

"What I'm going to do is stay here a few more years, collect a nice pension and leave Washington for good," Blake had said. "As for the health care system, I don't know what you can do. I don't know what anybody can do."

Senator Blake had gotten up slowly and left the room. He never discussed health care with Nancy again.

How This Book Differs from Other Books on Health Policy

In the brief account of the Wilson family, we met people who had interacted with the health care system—from patient to physician, hospital administrator to equipment manufacturer, employer to politician. In each vignette there were also unseen actors whose behavior was vitally important. The problems we encountered were wide-ranging—from how government should spend its health care dollars to how hospitals, insurance companies, employers, and even patients make important decisions. In some cases, it was clear that too much was being spent and resources were being wasted. In other cases, too little was being spent, sometimes at the cost of human life.

Yet one common denominator united each of the Wilson family's experiences and distinguished those experiences from what happens in other sectors of our economy: when individuals pursued their own interests, bad consequences resulted for other people.

In the current health care system, when individuals make socially bad decisions, the cost of those decisions often is borne by others, not by the decisionmaker. Conversely, when people make socially good decisions, most of the benefits of those decisions go to others. On the whole, people neither bear the full costs nor reap the full benefits of their decisions. As a consequence, the health care sector is replete with perverse incentives. Most of the time, what's good for the individual decisionmaker is bad for everyone else, and vice versa.

In most other sectors of our economy, individuals who make decisions realize most of the benefit from good ones and bear most of the cost of bad ones. To be sure, almost everything individuals do affects others, so the link between personal and social benefits is rarely perfect. Nonetheless, in most markets perverse incentives have been eliminated. The market for health care could be organized in a similar way.

In this book we depart substantially from previous works on public policy toward health care. The principal point of departure is the construction of two visions of the medical marketplace and the central role we assign to the individual pursuit of self-interest in each vision. The first is a vision of the medical marketplace as it operates now. The second is a vision of the medical marketplace as it can and should operate.

Aside from economists who produce purely technical works, most writers view the medical marketplace as primarily altruistic and charitable. The role of self-interest is rarely discussed. The word "market" is commonly avoided, as is the word "business." In most cases, the writers have been impressed by the fact that the health care sector is dominated by nonprofit institutions, which people mistakenly assume are characterized by selfless goals.

The few writers who have introduced the notion of self-interest have done so in the context of creating villains (for example, politicians, the American Medical Association, insurance companies, and hospital administrators). In their approach, greed has been assumed to intrude on a sector that is otherwise charitable and altruistic.

However, in this book, we accept self-interest as a normal characteristic of human behavior. Pursuit of self-interest is no more or less common in health care than in any other sector. The fact that some of our most important health care institutions are nonprofit (for example, medical schools, most hospitals, and many insurance companies and nursing homes) does not change human nature. That people actively pursue their own interests is not a bad thing. It is simply a fact. What matters most in the health care sector are the institutional arrangements under which self-interest is pursued.

Clearly, all of the principals in our Wilson family vignettes were self-interested. They made decisions that benefited them personally, even when their decisions subsequently hurt others. At the same time, none of the principals were greedy, mean-spirited, or indifferent to the suffering of others. There were no villains in this drama.

Not only did the characters pursue their own interests, but in most cases they believed they had little choice about doing so—and they were right. If Bob Wilson had known that Mr. Hansen was going to die the next day, undoubtedly he would have made an exception to the rules and admitted Hansen to the hospital. But he didn't know, and changing the rules for all patients would have increased hospital costs without increasing revenue. Too many decisions like that, and the hospital's board of directors would be looking for a new administrator. If Kay Pierce, the physician, had known that Irene Wilson had cancer, she would have behaved differently. But she didn't know, and giving free tests to all Medicare patients would probably have bankrupted her practice. Senator Blake might have been able to make minor changes in the system. But if he had tried to make radical changes, he wouldn't have been reelected. Mark Wilson might have been able to continue his employees' health insurance a bit longer. But ultimately, his uncompetitive costs would have forced him out of business.

Pursuit of self-interest, then, is much more than a natural characteristic of human behavior. In most institutional settings, it is a survival requirement. The institutional setting, however, determines whether our pursuit of self-interest is primarily beneficial or harmful to others. In regulated markets dominated by bureaucratic institutions, the interests of individuals frequently conflict. One person's gain is another's loss. More for me means less for you, and vice versa. In such an environment, when others pursue their interests, you and I are often made worse off.

Quite a different result emerges in competitive markets with clearly defined private property rights and individual freedom of choice. In that environment, you and I cannot pursue our own interests (for the most part) without creating benefits for others. Conversely, others rarely can pursue their interests without creating benefits for us.

Health Care Delivery as It Can and Should Be

Consider how differently the Wilson family would have fared in a world in which the medical marketplace works at least as well as the market for other complex services, and the market for health insurance works at least as well as the market for other kinds of insurance.

Jeff Wilson's Surgery

If the medical marketplace worked the way other markets do, Jeff Wilson would pay for his surgery with his own money. It might be money he had saved or money he had received from his health insurer once his condition had been diagnosed. But the money would belong to Jeff Wilson and he—not some remote bureaucracy—would be the principal buyer. In all probability, Jeff would choose outpatient surgery, the less expensive option. But if he chose inpatient surgery, the hospital would behave quite differently from the way hospitals operate today.

Before admitting Jeff, the hospital probably would give him a single package price covering all services. He could then compare it to the prices of competing hospitals. Few hospitals would refuse to state their prices in advance or present unreadable statements at the time of discharge. Hospitals that did those things would have mostly empty beds.

June Wilson's Headaches

If the health insurance market worked the way other insurance markets work, it is highly unlikely that June Wilson would receive any insurance money for headaches.

Health insurance would be restricted to rare, unusual events that have very costly consequences. Because using health insurance to pay small medical bills for routine services is costly and wasteful, June Wilson would use her own money to pay for most physicians' visits and diagnostic tests. If June's insurer did pay her some money for headaches, it would be hers to spend as she chose. Given her initial reaction to her doctor's questions, it is unlikely that she would pay for an MRI scan. If she did, she certainly would not check into a hospital.

George Wilson's Pacemaker

As would Jeff and June Wilson, George Wilson would be spending his own money. A large part of what he spent would come from the insurance check he received once his heart problem was diagnosed. But he might also have to use some of his savings.

Because George, not an insurance company, would be the customer, pacemaker manufacturers would seek him out. Higher quality pacemakers would still cost more, so George would have to evaluate the risks and the costs. Certainly he would consult his physician. But because the insurance company would no longer be the principal client, his doctor's advice would be far more informative and complete.

Irene Wilson's X-ray

If Medicare insurance worked the way most other insurance works, Medicare would be irrelevant in Irene's life unless she were diagnosed with a major illness. At that point she would receive a check. In the meantime, Medicare would not care whether Irene coughed or didn't cough, and her doctor would have no forms on which to report such trivia.

Her doctor would be in the business of selling services, and if Irene chose to purchase chest x-rays, she would be spending her own money. Because Irene, not Medicare, would be the customer, her doctor would have an incentive to encourage her to have an annual chest x-ray, especially in view of her smoking history. Irene could also solicit advice from other physicians. In all probability, x-ray machine manufacturers would advertise directly to people such as Irene—since Medicare would no longer be their client either. Odds are that Irene would receive encouragement from many sources to get the annual x-ray. The choice would be hers.

Mr. Hansen's Hospital Admission

If the medical marketplace functioned as other markets do, when Mr. Hansen got to the emergency room he, not Medicare, would be the hospital's potential customer. If he entered the hospital, he would be spending his own money, for his condition.

The Hansen family may not have much money. But Hansen was not on Medicaid, so he probably was not living in poverty. Hansen and his family might have been a hard sell. But a hospital in a competitive medical marketplace would be in the business of selling services to people, not insurers, and in the Hansen case the argument for immediate hospitalization would be very persuasive. At the very minimum, the Hansen family would make an informed choice.

Group Insurance for Mark Wilson's Employees

If the health insurance market were freely competitive (or at least as free of regulatory obstacles as the market for life, fire, and casualty insurance), state legislators would not tell Mark Wilson what to include in his company's group health insurance plan. Mark and his employees would simply agree on an affordable package of benefits. The employees might have to forgo some frills, but they would still have catastrophic insurance.

The problems that Mark and his employees had with government under the present system did not end with the state legislature. Federal tax law also interfered. If Mark's company purchased the insurance, it could pay with pretax dollars. But if employees purchased insurance on their own, they had to pay with aftertax dollars. If federal tax law had been designed for individuals rather than for companies, it would have permitted a full range of options for each employee. In that case, not all employees would be forced to accept the same package of health insurance benefits. Each could choose among competing health insurance plans and purchase the policy with nontaxed dollars (the same way their employers do now).

Making Senator Blake's Life Easier

Senator Blake's principal problem stemmed from the federal government's attempts to do something of which it is incapable: operate a giant insurance company. Moreover, as has private insurance, Medicare insurance has long since ceased to be genuine insurance—it is instead prepayment for the consumption of medical care. Thus, Senator Blake and his colleagues must decide who gets to consume what and how much—an unpleasant task.

To make matters worse, decisionmakers such as Blake are continually pressured by special interests. Not surprisingly, by the time all of the pressures have sorted themselves out, Medicare has violated every principle of sound insurance. That is not unusual. In every field in which the government operates an insurance program, sound insurance principles are sacrificed to political pressures.

Is there a way of replacing Medicare with a program that takes advantage of private-sector strengths in providing the elderly with health care? Yes—and at least one country, Singapore, has made substantial progress toward implementing a totally private system.

The market for medical care will never be exactly like the market for corn or wheat, but there is no reason why we cannot create a similar institutional framework. We can transfer the power to make important decisions from large institutions such as government, corporate employers, insurance companies, and hospitals to individuals. We can allow supply, demand, and competition to allocate resources. Consumer preference and individual choice can determine the ultimate form of our health care system.

2.
Our Present Health Care System

In a normal market, problems are solved by individual initiative on the part of consumers and producers pursuing their own self-interest. Consumers circumvent waste, inefficiency, and resulting high prices by searching for good products at attractive prices offered by efficient suppliers. Producers search for less costly ways of meeting consumer needs. Pursuit of self-interest by consumers rewards the most efficient producers, and pursuit of self-interest by producers rewards consumers.

In the health care sector, however, normal market processes have been replaced by bureaucratic institutions and normal market incentives by bureaucratic rule making. As a result, the scope for individual initiative is greatly restricted, and often people can pursue their own interests only by creating costs for others. For example:

- Whereas consumers in a normal market spend their own money, in the medical marketplace consumers are usually spending someone else's money. Only 5 cents of every dollar of hospital income and only 19 cents of each dollar of physicians' fees is paid by patients using their own funds.
- Whereas individuals in other insurance markets may choose from diverse products, the vast majority of people who have health insurance are covered under an employer or government plan. Despite so-called cafeteria options, an individual usually can-

not purchase a less expensive plan with a different type of coverage without making considerable personal sacrifice.

- Whereas innovation and technological change in a normal market are viewed as good for consumers, third-party payers in the medical marketplace are increasingly hostile to new technology and discourage its development.
- Whereas producers in a normal market advertise price discounts and quality differences, most patients in the hospital marketplace cannot find out what the cost will be prior to admission and cannot read the hospital bill upon discharge. Patients rarely can obtain information about the quality of physicians or hospitals, even when quality problems are well-known within the medical community.

The result is a marketplace in which the pursuit of self-interest often does not solve problems; it creates them instead. When consumers consume, they drive up insurance premium costs for other consumers. The primary ways in which physicians and hospitals increase their incomes also lead to increasing insurance premiums. Rarely can individuals act to change things without operating through large bureaucracies, and when bureaucracies attempt solutions, their "success" usually creates new problems and new costs for other bureaucracies.

How America's Health Care Crisis Evolved

In most Western industrial democracies, health care systems shaped by government policies have evolved through three stages.

The Cost-Plus System of Health Care Finance (Stage I)

From the end of World War II through the mid-1980s, Americans paid for hospital care principally through a cost-plus system of health care finance. Cost-plus reimbursement worked like this: If Blue Cross patients accounted for 25 percent of a hospital's patient days, Blue Cross reimbursed the hospital for 25 percent of its total costs. If Medicare patients accounted for 30 percent of the hospital's patient days, Medicare paid the hospital 30 percent. Other insurers reimbursed in much the same way.[1] Health insurance literally ensured that hospitals had enough income to cover their costs, and health insurers acted as agents not for their policyholders but for the suppliers of medical services. Because the only way the suppliers could increase their incomes was to increase costs, the cost-plus system invariably led to rising health care costs.

A cost-plus system could never exist if patients were spending their own money in a competitive marketplace. Therefore, the prerequisite for cost-plus medicine was a market in which the supply side was dominated by nonprofit institutions that competed in only limited ways. The demand side was dominated by large, third-party bureaucracies that were more responsive to the needs of sellers of medical services than to the needs of the insured. By the 1970s, those institutions were firmly in place.[2]

In a cost-plus system, the pressures to increase spending on health care were inexorable. Patients had no reason to show restraint, since the funds they spent belonged not to them but to third-party institutions. When they entered the medical marketplace, they were spending someone else's money, not their own.

Physicians often believed that the "pure" practice of medicine could and should be free from the constraints of money. In prescribing tests and other medical treatments,

[1] See John C. Goodman and Gerald L. Musgrave, *The Changing Market for Health Insurance: Opting Out of the Cost-Plus System,* NCPA Policy Report no. 118 (Dallas: National Center for Policy Analysis, September 1985).

[2] For an analysis of how those institutions evolved, see John C. Goodman, *The Regulation of Medical Care: Is the Price Too High?* (Washington: Cato Institute, 1980). A different perspective, one more sympathetic to the suppression of market incentives, is presented in Paul Starr, *The Social Transformation of American Medicine* (New York: Basic Books, 1982).

physicians not only did not think about costs, they had no idea what those costs were. Guided by the sole consideration of patient health, physicians were inclined to do anything and everything that might help the patient—restrained only by the ethical injunction to do no harm.

The system in its pure cost-plus phase rewarded scientists, inventors, and research and development personnel. The message of the medical marketplace was, "Invent it, show us it will improve health, and we will buy it, regardless of the cost."

The role of the hospital was to provide an environment in which cost-plus medicine could be practiced, in which all of the latest technology was available, within easy reach and on demand. In such a world, hospital administrators did not manage doctors. On the contrary, they served the physicians' interest in practicing medicine by interfering as little as possible in the physicians' activities.

Such a hospital environment would be inconceivable were it not for a system that reimbursed hospitals on the basis of their costs. The role of third-party payers in the system, therefore, was to pay whatever bills were submitted, with few questions asked. Cost increases were passed along to policyholders in the form of higher health insurance premiums.

The Cost-Plus System in Its Cost-Control Phase (Stage II)

Because there is a limit to how much any society will pay for health care, the cost-plus system was ultimately forced to limit the decisions of the suppliers of medical care in arbitrary ways. The limitations took the form of rules and restrictions written by impersonal bureaucracies, far removed from the doctor-patient relationships they sought to regulate.

During the 1980s, the U.S. health care system evolved from a pure cost-plus system (Stage I) into a cost-plus system in its cost-control phase (Stage II). In this second stage, there are many different third-party paying institutions, some public and some private. Each is engaged in a bureaucratic struggle—not merely to resist the cost-plus push of the medical care providers, but also to reduce its share of the total cost. Each separate third-party institution is free to initiate its own cost-control strategy in random and uncoordinated ways. But since the basic structure of cost-plus finance has not changed (that is, no real market has been created), Stage II only secondarily is about holding down total spending. Primarily, it is about bureaucratic warfare over shifting costs.

The central focus of third-party paying institutions is on eliminating "waste." Yet bureaucratic institutions (operating principally through reimbursement strategies chosen by people remote from actual patients and doctors) usually cannot eliminate waste without harming patients. Third-party payers may seek to eliminate waste by controlling price or quantity, or both. By the very act of trying to control prices, however, they invariably focus on a normal price for a normal service, ignoring patients and institutional settings that are not normal. In the very act of trying to control quantity (for example, by eliminating "unnecessary" surgery or "unnecessary" hospital admissions), they again invariably set standards for what is normal—ignoring the unanticipated, abnormal circumstances in which medical care is often delivered.

On the supply side of the medical marketplace, institutions have great resources and considerable experience at resisting change. So, in the face of a cost-control measure initiated by one institutional buyer, the suppliers attempt to shift costs to another, without changing their fundamental behavior. The suppliers are sufficiently adept at this so that, over the long haul, costs are not really controlled in Stage II. At best, each new wave of buyer restrictions slows the rate of increase. But after suppliers adjust to the new restrictions, costs rise again. Precisely for that reason, a system in Stage II evolves into Stage III. It is in this final stage that institutional buyers acquire the ultimate weapon in the cost-control battle—the power of government.

Evolution to National Health Insurance (Stage III)

In the final phase of the cost-plus system's evolution, third-party payers directly or indirectly control the entire system. They begin to determine what technology can be used, what constitutes ethical behavior in the practice of medicine, even what illnesses can be treated and how. Ultimately, they determine who lives and who dies.

In this third stage, government not only controls the total amount of spending on health care but also actively intervenes in the allocation of health care dollars. Stage III is pure special-interest warfare, fought out in the political arena. It takes all of the struggles present in Stage II and elevates them to the realm of politics.

How the Cost-Plus System Affects Patients

In Stage I of the evolution of a cost-plus system, the quality of medical care delivered may be very high. That is because medical care is administered in an environment in which cost is no object, and physicians are trained to do everything possible to alleviate any and all illnesses, real or imagined. Once the system enters its cost-control phase, however, the quality of care can deteriorate rapidly. That is because competing institutions begin a monumental struggle over resources. In this environment, the patient is no longer seen as a consumer or buyer of medical care. Indeed, individual patients are largely unimportant except insofar as their formal consent is needed to legitimize the bureaucratic warfare over vast sums of money.

The Role of Insurance

Outside of the health care sector, there are well-developed markets for insurance for a wide variety of unforeseen, risky events: life insurance (for an unforeseen death), automobile liability insurance (for an unforeseen automobile accident), fire and casualty insurance (for unforeseen damage to property), and disability insurance (for unforeseen physical injuries). Indeed, there is hardly any risk that is not, in principle, insurable. Lloyd's of London will even insure against the failure of a communications satellite to achieve orbit, and it wrote coverage for ships in the Persian Gulf and off the coast of Israel from the day Operation Desert Storm began.

All of those markets have certain common characteristics.[3] The amount to be reimbursed is based on a risky event. Once the event has occurred and the damage has been assessed, the insurer writes a check to the policyholder for the agreed-upon amount. Policyholders are free to do whatever they wish with the money they receive.

In the market for health insurance, however, things are very different. Often, there need not be any risky event to trigger insurance payments. (June Wilson, for example, had had tension headaches for years.) Once it is determined that a health insurer owes something, the amount to be paid is not a predetermined sum but is instead determined by the consumption decisions of the policyholder. (Jeff Wilson, for example, chose to have surgery in a hospital rather than as an outpatient, and June Wilson elected to undergo a battery of tests.) Finally, payment is made not to the insured but to medical providers, based on the consumption decisions that are made.[4] Those differences shape the way the health insurance market functions. In fact, in many respects health insurance is not insurance at all. It is instead prepayment for the consumption of medical care.

Because health insurance is the primary method of payment for the medical services Americans consume, in a very real sense it is the insurer rather than the patient who is the customer of medical providers. Thus, June Wilson and Jeff Wilson were not the principal buyers of the medical care they received. Blue Cross was. Similarly, Irene Wilson and

---

[3] An exception is insurance for tort liabilities, which has many of the defects of health insurance and leads to many of the same problems.

[4] There are a few exceptions, such as policies that indemnify patients in the form of a fixed sum of money per day spent in the hospital for a procedure or a diagnosis (for example, cancer).

Mr. Hansen were not the principal buyers of their medical care. Medicare was.

The Relationship between Buyer and Seller

In a normal marketplace, buyers and sellers negotiate over price, quantity, quality, and other terms for big-ticket items or important transactions. For smaller, frequent, and less critical transactions, buyers search for the most favorable terms or conditions. Sellers adjust terms and conditions to meet customers' needs and to react to the offers of their rivals. An exchange is not consummated unless it benefits both parties. The preferences of other people, not parties to the exchange, are rarely considered. In the medical marketplace, however, things are very different.

In reflecting on the experiences of the hypothetical Wilson family, it is interesting to note that there was never a real exchange. That is, there was no case in which a buyer and seller reached a mutually beneficial agreement, independent of the wishes of others. To the contrary, in every case an entity (for example, government or an insurance company) not a party to the exchange was far more important in determining what ultimately happened than the parties who interacted.

In the cases of Jeff, June, and George Wilson, the medical procedures performed were far more influenced by the reimbursement policies of private insurers than by any mutually beneficial exchange between patients and their doctors. In the cases of Irene Wilson and Mr. Hansen, what was done or not done was virtually unaffected by the preferences of the patients and their families. Instead, the decisions of the medical providers were determined exclusively by the Medicare bureaucracy.

When the legislators in some distant city decided what elements had to be contained in a group health insurance policy, none of them asked Mark Wilson or his employees what their preferences were. So, unlike their counterparts at Williams, Inc., Mark Wilson and his employees never had the opportunity to find a scaled-down policy that the company could afford. The decision to end group health insurance at Mark Wilson's company was not a mutually beneficial agreement between employer and employees. It was an outcome dictated by politicians who didn't even know Mark Wilson and the people who worked for him.

In the medical marketplace, rules imposed by third-party institutions increasingly shape medical practice. When Medicare patients interact with the health care system, what procedures are performed—and whether a procedure is performed—is determined more by reimbursement rules than by patient preferences or the physician's experience and judgment. Although that phenomenon is more evident in government health care programs (Medicare and Medicaid), private insurers and large companies are increasingly copying the methods of government.

The Role of Information

One of the most striking things about the Wilson family's experiences is how little information the people had. Those making decisions lacked not only information about the monetary cost of their decisions but often the information that could have saved their lives.

Consider the differences between the experiences of the Wilson family and our everyday experiences in non-health-care markets. Jeff Wilson agreed to hospital surgery with no idea what it would cost him. When he was discharged, he was presented with a statement that he could not read or understand. He assumed Blue Cross would look out for his interests, but he had no idea how Blue Cross handled claims. Unquestionably, there is no other market in which Jeff Wilson could be a buyer (including the market for any other type of insurance) in which anything even remotely similar takes place.

In almost every other market, the biggest problem that sellers have is getting information to prospective buyers. Those who have a better product or a better way to meet consumer needs often go to great expense to convey the information to potential customers. But in the experiences of the Wilson family, precisely the reverse was true. In fact, in example after example, essential information was intentionally concealed and withheld.

George Wilson, for example, had no idea that his pacemaker was not of the highest quality or that better products existed. The person in the best position to tell him about the options (his physician) didn't do so. Irene Wilson, who died of lung cancer, did not understand how Medicare works. She didn't know that there were services that she could and should have been purchasing with her own money. Again, the person in the best position to tell her (her physician) failed to do so. In all probability, when Mr. Hansen came to the emergency room, no one explained to the Hansen family the options and the probable costs and risks associated with each.

Why is vitally important information persistently withheld and concealed in the medical marketplace? Because in the health care sector, people discover that it is in their self-interest to withhold information. In general, medical equipment manufacturers, pharmaceutical companies, and other suppliers with information about quality do not communicate the information to patients because they do not view patients as the principal buyers. Their principal customers are hospitals, physicians, and third-party institutions. Patients frequently do not have information about quality for yet another reason. In an effort to suppress competition among providers, associations of physicians and hospitals have made it difficult, if not impossible, for patients to get information about quality. Avoiding quality comparisons has become a matter of professional ethics. In the past, adherence to such ethical codes was backed by the force of state law. As a result, in most communities patients cannot even discover the mortality rate for surgery and for specific surgeons at public hospitals funded by the patients' own tax dollars.

3.
Vision of an Ideal Health Care System

Before we recommend solutions to America's health care problems, we need a clear idea of where we want to go. Our vision, which we call Patient Power, is of a health care system in which patient choice and competitive market forces are restored to their proper central role. The Patient Power vision does not look to an ideal world in which there are no problems. Instead, Patient Power envisions a medical marketplace that simply works at least as well as most other markets in which we buy and sell.

Goals of the Patient Power Vision

We can identify five goals of the Patient Power vision. By the very act of reaching these goals, we would simultaneously be solving America's health care problems. Specifically, an ideal system would seek to:

- Transfer power from large institutions and impersonal bureaucracies to individuals.
- Restore the buyer-seller relationship to patients and medical suppliers, so that patients (rather than third-party insurers) become the principal buyers of health care.
- Create institutions in which patients (as much as possible) spend their own money, rather than someone else's, when they purchase health care.
- Remove health care (as much as possible) from the political arena, in which well-organized special

interests can cause great harm to the rest of us.
- Subject the health care sector to the rigors of competition and create market-based institutions in which individuals reap the full benefits of their good decisions and bear the full cost of their bad ones.

How Patient Power Would Function

In a health care system designed to pursue the goals listed above, the roles of patients, physicians, hospitals, insurance companies, employers, and even government would be radically different. The principal differences would be that:

- Patients rather than third-party payers would become the principal buyers of health care, with opportunities to compare options, compare prices, and make decisions.
- Physicians would no longer serve primarily as the agents of third-party payers but would serve as the agents of patients and help them to make informed choices.
- Hospitals would no longer serve primarily as the agents of either physicians or third-party payers but would become competitors in the business of health care delivery and would compete for patients by improving quality and lowering prices.
- Health insurance companies would no longer be buyers of health care but would specialize in the business of insurance and reimburse policyholders in the case of unforeseen and risky adverse health events.
- Employers would not be buyers of health care and would not make decisions for employees concerning their health insurance but would be agents for individual employees and help them to make informed choices and to monitor the performance of competing insurers.

- Government—in its role as an insurer of last resort—would no longer serve as a buyer of health care but would pay health insurance premiums for indigent policyholders.
- Government—in its policymaking role—would facilitate the goals of the system on the demand side by encouraging private savings for small medical bills, private health insurance for large medical bills, and life-long savings for medical needs during retirement; on the supply side, government would encourage free and open competition in the markets for physicians' services, hospital services, and private health insurance.

The Health Care System of Singapore

To see one way in which a market-based health care system might work, it is worth examining Singapore's health care system, which is part of a much wider system based on an explicit goal: no government subsidies. The philosophy of Singapore is: Each individual should pay his or her own way; each family should pay its own way; and each generation should pay its own way. Government transfers should be minimal. Progress toward that goal has been remarkable. Over the last decade, savings account balances have soared and government spending on traditional welfare programs has decreased dramatically.

The government of Singapore has attempted to identify all of the major needs that other governments approach with welfare and entitlement programs and to meet those needs by requiring people to save. In Singapore, personal savings accounts are replacing the welfare state.

For example, instead of a government-run social security system, Singapore's residents are required to save for their own retirement. Instead of a government-run health care system, people are required to place 6 percent of their annual income in medical savings accounts. Funds build up in those accounts tax-free and can be spent only on medical care. The program of forced savings also covers other needs. Required (retirement) savings can be used to buy life insurance and disability insurance, make a down payment on a home, or finance a child's college education.

With respect to health care, the Singapore system makes sure that money spent on medical services is in the hands of the consumers of those services. In general, 6 percent of a person's income over an entire working life will pay for hospitalization for the vast majority of medical episodes that can occur, and only recently has Singapore introduced catastrophic health insurance to pay large medical bills.

In 1955, Singapore introduced a compulsory savings program that now covers about three-fourths of all Singaporean workers. Employer and employee contributions are made to the Central Provident Fund (CPF), which is controlled by the government and has a monopoly status. In the beginning, the CPF invested its funds entirely in government securities, and withdrawals were essentially limited to lump-sum retirement benefits or survivors benefits. Over the years, the program has acquired flexibility. Workers can now direct the investment of up to 40 percent of their CPF funds and can withdraw funds to purchase a home, buy life insurance, or buy home mortgage insurance; and they can borrow funds from their accounts to pay college education expenses for a family member.

All employees in Singapore have a private property right to the funds that accumulate in their individual CPF accounts. The funds may be withdrawn at retirement, in the event of permanent disability, or if the individual emigrates from Singapore. At the account holder's death, the funds are payable to the individual's heirs.

Beginning in 1984, the government of Singapore extended its program of forced savings to require that a certain portion of CPF contributions be put into "medical savings accounts" to provide funds for hospitalization. The funds may be used only for treatment at a government hospital or an approved private hospital. Strangely, medical savings account funds cannot be used to purchase outpatient care, including physicians' services or expensive outpatient renal dialysis and long-term care. People also cannot borrow against future medical savings account deposits to pay current bills at private hospitals, although members of the same family can pool their medical savings account balances to pay another family member's hospital bill, and people who enter some government hospitals can settle their bills from future medical savings account deposits.

Currently, 6 percent of an employee's salary is placed in a medical savings account until the balance reaches approximately $8,522. Once that total is reached and maintained, any additional contributions are automatically placed in an individual's ordinary pension account. In Singapore, $8,522 would be sufficient to cover hospitalization expenses except in very rare catastrophic cases. The Singapore government currently is engaged in negotiations with private health insurance companies and is apparently committed to allowing some portion of the medical savings account funds to be used for the purchase of health insurance coverage. In 1985, 145,000 members of the CPF (of a total Singapore population of 2.6 million) made medical savings account withdrawals averaging about $171 per person. The use of medical savings account funds quadrupled between 1985 and 1988.

The Singaporean system is far from perfect. Restrictions on the use of medical savings account funds encourage people to overuse hospital care and underuse less expensive alternatives. Certain restrictions favor public over private hospitals (although Singapore now is privatizing its public hospitals) and discourage the development of a competitive market for hospital care. And some restrictions against borrowing from future medical savings account deposits to pay current expenses seem unwise, since medical expenses cannot be timed to match the buildup of medical savings account funds. On the other hand, Singapore already has developed one of the most innovative ways of paying for health care found anywhere in the world—a vast system of individual self-insurance.

As a further benefit of the Singapore system, Singaporeans can use excess balances in their pension and medical savings accounts to help finance the purchase of a home. Bruce Knecht, writing in *Barron's,* points out that "more than 90 percent of Singaporeans own their own homes, more than in any other country."[1] That developing nation is achieving, with pro-market ideas, what seems to be only a luxurious dream for American social planners. It's too bad that young Americans can't look forward to high quality, affordable health care, home ownership, and retirement checks at age 55. Those are all de facto rights in Singapore, brought about not by tax and spend, but by individual work and thrift. While we certainly do not support the compulsory nature of Singapore's programs, and the lack of freedom in much of the rest of Singaporean society, Americans should at least consider how they can achieve similar results.

Can Patients Function as Informed Consumers in the Medical Marketplace?

The most common public objection to using markets to solve health care problems relates to the complexity of medical decisions and the inability of patients to make wise choices. Medical science is complicated and becoming more so. Moreover, most medical episodes (such as gall bladder malfunction) occur only once in a person's lifetime. Given that, for any one person, such episodes occur infrequently, individual patients cannot be expected to learn from experience or to invest much time, energy, and money in learning about a medical procedure on the slight chance that they may need it some day. How then, even under the best of circumstances, can patients make wise decisions about whether to have gall bladder surgery, what physician to use, and what hospital to enter?

[1] G. Bruce Knecht, "Government Stars in Singapore's Show," *Barron's,* August 23, 1993.

The answer is that they must rely on the advice of others. Short of going to medical school themselves, there is no alternative. However, the fact that we must depend on others for advice does not mean that we should surrender power to them.

The primary difference between markets and nonmarket bureaucracies is consumer sovereignty. In general, the more complicated a market, the stronger the case for consumers' not surrendering the power to make ultimate decisions. If choosing a physician is complex, choosing a politician who will appoint a bureaucrat to choose a physician is even more complex. Elevating choices to the realm of politics only makes the choices harder. In selecting a politician, we consumers would not simply be selecting a doctor-chooser; we would be selecting a person who would make many other decisions affecting our lives. If choosing the wrong doctor can cause harm, then choosing the wrong politician to choose the doctor for us can cause even more harm. What is true of politicians is also true of employers, insurance companies, and any other bureaucracy.

Imagine you live in a country with national health insurance, in which health care is routinely and arbitrarily rationed by the medical bureaucracy. Knowing the institutional setting, you are predisposed to distrust the advice you receive from a physician. If told that you do not need an expensive diagnostic test or surgical procedure, you have no way of knowing whether the advice represents state-of-the-art medicine or potentially lethal rationing. Discovering whether you really need an expensive procedure is only half the problem. Once you know you need it, you still have to cope with the complexities of bureaucratic rationing. Getting to the head of the line is, in itself, a skill and an art. Unless you are willing to totally give up control and do whatever physicians tell you, your problems in a bureaucratic system are even more complex than in a market system.

An important principle to remember is: No one cares more about you and your family than you do. And the further removed decisionmakers are from you and your family—geographically, economically, and politically—the less likely they are to make the same decision you would have made with respect to your health care. Another important principle is: We can often take advantage of the wisdom and experience of others without transferring power to them. If politicians have wise advice to give, we can take their advice while retaining the ultimate authority to make our own decisions.

Precisely because the medical marketplace is complex, employers, insurance companies, governments, health organizations, and nonprofit entities collect and assimilate information that no single patient (or physician) would ever collect. The concept behind "managed care," for example, is that organizations can collect information and use it to raise the quality and reduce the cost of medical care—especially with respect to complicated and expensive procedures. Whether the goal is reached depends on the institutional environment. In a market-based system, organizations that specialize in collecting information can be valuable to both patients and physicians. In a bureaucratic system, such organizations are used to control the behavior of patients and physicians. One system uses information to help people reach their own goals, the other to prevent them from doing so.

In market-based systems, people find it in their self-interest to communicate information to consumers. In bureaucracies, the reverse is true. The more information consumers have, the harder life is for bureaucrats. Dissemination of knowledge is good for the life of markets—it makes them work better—but it is bad for the life of bureaucracies.

The U.S. health care system is far more bureaucratic than most people know. Yet there are welcome signs of change. The cover story of a 1990 issue of *U.S. News & World Report* was entitled "America's Best Hospitals: A National Guide That Helps You Choose."[2] The fact that the article

---

[2] *U.S. News & World Report*, April 30, 1990.

was a cover story shows how rare and unusual it is for such information to be communicated to the general public. A recent book published by Consumers Union (also the publisher of *Consumer Reports)* is entitled *The Savvy Patient: How to Be an Active Participant in Your Medical Care.*[3]

The most important conclusion that follows from the observation that the medical marketplace is complex is the necessity of creating an institutional environment in which "experts" will find it in their self-interest to give us accurate information and wise advice. And the best way to create that environment is to empower patients by giving them greater control over health care dollars.

Reforming the American Health Care System

We cannot dismantle the current health care system overnight. We can move in the right direction, however, by adopting policies that promote the development of a competitive system and by eliminating policies that make such a system unattainable. The Patient Power agenda described in this chapter is designed to remove harmful, government-created obstacles and to create new incentives under which people will be encouraged to solve problems through individual initiative and choice. Specifically, this agenda would:

- Give individuals greater opportunity to choose among competing health insurance plans and to select the type of coverage best suited to their individual and family needs.
- Give individuals the opportunity to choose between employer-provided group health insurance and individual or family policies—without income tax penalties.
- Give individuals the opportunity to choose between self-insurance and third-party insurance

[3] David R. Stutz, Bernard Feder, and the editors of Consumer Reports Books, *The Savvy Patient: How to Be an Active Participant in Your Medical Care* (Mount Vernon, N.Y.: Consumer Reports Books, 1990).

for small medical bills—without income tax penalties.

- Give individuals the opportunity to choose health insurance plans with effective cost-control techniques and to realize the financial benefits from making such choices—without income tax penalties.
- Give individuals the opportunity to build a reserve of savings for future medical expenses, so that they can rely less on third-party insurance and reduce their annual health insurance premiums.

Establishing Equity in Taxation

Under current law, health insurance provided by an employer is excluded from the taxable wages of the employees, but insurance premiums paid by individuals are not tax deductible. Consequently, some people realize generous tax advantages from the purchase of health insurance, while others do not. A reasonable solution is to grant the same tax treatment with respect to health insurance to all Americans, regardless of employment and regardless of who purchases the health insurance policy—an individual, an employer or a self-employed person.

As Figure 3.1 shows, workers in the 28 percent federal income tax bracket face a marginal tax rate of 43.3 percent, leaving them with less than 57 cents in take-home pay out of each additional dollar of earnings. If state and local income taxes also apply, the situation is much worse. Indeed, millions of American workers take home less than 50 cents of each dollar of earnings. Such high tax rates give employers and employees strong incentives to replace wages with nontaxable health insurance benefits, even if health insurance would not otherwise have been purchased. The total tax deduction for employer-provided health insurance is about $60 billion per year, or roughly $600 for every American family. Yet most of the 37 million individuals who do not have health insurance (including about 18.8 million with a

Figure 3.1
TAKE-HOME PAY FROM AN ADDITIONAL DOLLAR OF WAGES*

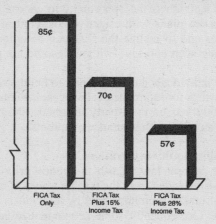

* Includes employer's share of FICA taxes.

family member in the workforce)[4] and about 12 percent of insured individuals who purchase health insurance on their own receive no tax subsidy. As a result, some employees of large companies have lavish health insurance, totally tax deductible, while other Americans have none.

In general, the value of the right to exclude health insurance coverage from taxable wages ranges from about $1,200 per year in reduced taxes for an auto worker to about $300 for a worker in the retail trade.[5] Yet self-employed individuals, the unemployed, and employees of firms that do not provide health insurance receive little or no tax deduction for the health insurance they purchase. Not sur-

---

[4] Jill D. Foley, *Uninsured in the United States: The Nonelderly Population without Health Insurance* (Washington: Employee Benefit Research Institute, April 1991), Table 1.

[5] Aldona Robbins and Gary Robbins, *What a Canadian-Style Health Care Scheme Would Cost U.S. Employers and Their Employees,* NCPA Policy Report no. 145 (Dallas: National Center for Policy Analysis, February 1990).

prisingly, people respond to such incentives. About 92 percent of Americans who have private health insurance acquired it through an employer.[6] The more generous the tax subsidy, the more likely people are to have health insurance. Those most likely to be uninsured are people who receive no tax subsidy.

If it is desirable for people to have health insurance, and if we care about equity, then all Americans should receive the same tax encouragement to purchase health insurance, regardless of employment. Accordingly, the self-employed, the unemployed, and employees who purchase health insurance on their own should be entitled to a tax deduction or tax credit that is just as generous as the tax treatment they would have received if their policies had been provided by an employer.

Equalizing Tax Advantages for Families with Unequal Incomes

Under the current system, the ability to exclude employer-provided health insurance from taxable income is more valuable to people in higher tax brackets. However, if it is socially desirable to use the income tax system to encourage families to purchase health insurance for large medical bills, then all families should receive the same encouragement.

For a low-income worker who is paying no income tax, federal tax law makes a dollar of health insurance benefits equivalent to $1.18 in wages. For a worker who is in the 28 percent bracket and paying the Social Security (FICA) tax, a dollar of health insurance benefits is equivalent to $1.76 in wages.[7] Because the value of the tax subsidy rises with income, it is hardly surprising that the lower a family's income, the less likely the family is to have health insurance.

[6] Foley, Table 17, pp. 46-47.

[7] The value of the benefit equals $1/(1-t)$, where t is the marginal federal income tax rate plus the combined employer-employee Social Security payroll tax rate. For a worker in the 15 percent bracket, $t = 0.15 + 0.153$. For a worker in the 28 percent bracket, $t = 0.28 + 0.153$.

Figure 3.2
PERCENTAGE OF NONELDERLY POPULATION COVERED BY
EMPLOYER-PROVIDED HEALTH INSURANCE, 1989

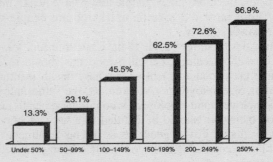

Income as a Percentage of Poverty Level

SOURCE: C. Eugene Steuerle, "Finance-Based Reform: The Search for an Adaptable Health Policy," Paper presented at an American Enterprise Institute conference, American Health Policy, Washington, October 3-4, 1991.

About 61 percent of all people who lack health insurance have annual incomes of less than $20,000.[8] As Figure 3.2 shows, about 87 percent of people with incomes at least 2.5 times the poverty level have employer-provided health insurance. Only a small fraction of those at or below the poverty level have it, however. As a result, the current system is highly regressive, conferring the largest subsidies on those families with the highest incomes. As Figure 3.3 shows, families in the top fifth of the income distribution receive an annual subsidy of about $1,560. By contrast, families in the bottom fifth receive an average annual subsidy of only $270.

To give all people the same economic incentives to purchase health insurance, premiums paid by employers should be included in the gross wages of their employees, and all taxpayers should receive a tax credit equal to, say,

[8] Foley. Not all people who lack health insurance have low incomes. About one-fifth have family incomes in excess of $30,000.

Figure 3.3

AVERAGE VALUE OF ANNUAL FEDERAL TAX SUBSIDIES FOR
EMPLOYER-PROVIDED HEALTH INSURANCE, 1992*

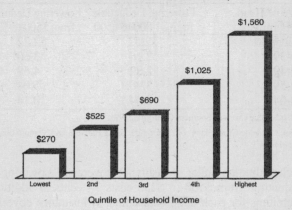

Quintile of Household Income

SOURCE: C. Eugene Steuerle, "Finance-Based Reform: The Search for an
Adaptable Health Policy," Paper presented at an American Enterprise Institute
conference, American Health Policy, Washington, October 3-4, 1991.

* Revenue loss includes both Social Security (FICA) and income taxes.

30 percent of the premium. That would make the tax subsidy for health insurance the same for all taxpayers, regardless of income and regardless of whether the policies are
purchased individually or by employers. For individuals
who pay no federal income tax, the tax credit could be
made refundable.

Creating Individual Self-Insurance for Small Medical Bills

The easiest way to hold down increases in health insurance premiums is to choose policies with high deductibles.
On a representative individual health insurance policy for a
middle-aged male, lowering the annual deductible from
$1,000 to $500 costs 64 cents in additional premiums for

Table 3.1

COST OF EACH ADDITIONAL DOLLAR OF HEALTH INSURANCE
COVERAGE IN CALIFORNIA*

Age of Head of Family	Lowering Deductible from $1,000 to $500	Lowering Deductible from $500 to $250
Under 30	$2.52	$2.22
30-39	2.16	3.60
40-49	2.82	4.68
50-59	3.90	5.04
60-64	2.04	10.14

SOURCE: Blue Cross of Southern California, 1991.

*Based on Blue Cross plans sold in Orange, Santa Barbara, and Ventura counties in early 1991.

each additional dollar of insurance coverage.[9] Lowering the deductible from $500 to $250 costs 74 cents in additional premiums for each additional dollar of insurance coverage. Although lower deductible policies may occasionally be a good buy for a particular individual, they cannot possibly be a good buy for policyholders as a group, who will pay far more in premiums than they will collect in medical benefits.

For people who live in high-cost areas, low-deductible health insurance is even more wasteful. Consider, for example, the costs of lowering the deductible on a Blue Cross family policy in California. As Table 3.1 shows, any deductible lower than $1,000 is a terrible buy unless federal tax law offsets the waste in the manner described above. Suppose a 40-year-old living in Orange County, California, has a Blue Cross family policy with a $250 deductible. If the family chose a $1,000 deductible instead, it would give up $600 of health insurance coverage (since Blue Cross pays only 80 percent of the additional $750 of expenses). But in return, the family would cut its health insurance premiums by $2,064! Savings of that magnitude are not typical.

[9] These calculations are based on policies sold by Golden Rule Insurance Company, the largest seller of individual and family health insurance policies in the country. Other insurance companies sell similar policies at similar prices.

However, the example illustrates dramatically that opportunities for saving do exist in the health insurance market.

Despite the fact that low-deductible insurance policies are often wasteful, tax law encourages such policies and discourages high-deductible policies. On a $1,000-deductible policy, for example, the first $1,000 must be paid out-of-pocket with aftertax dollars. If that $1,000 were paid by employer-provided insurance, the premium could be paid with pretax dollars.

To eliminate the perverse incentives in the current system, individuals should be allowed to choose higher deductibles and deposit the premium savings in personal medical savings accounts. Such accounts would serve as self-insurance for small medical bills. Medical savings accounts would be the private property of the account holders and become part of an individual's estate at the time of death. Contributions to medical savings accounts would receive the same tax encouragement as payments for conventional health insurance (see Chapter 5).

Creating individual and family medical savings accounts would represent a major departure from the current system of paying for health care. Those accounts would have immediate advantages that would become even more important over time. Because medical savings accounts would last an individual's entire life, they would allow people to engage in lifetime planning—recognizing that health and medical expenses are related to lifestyle. Moreover, medical savings accounts would eventually become an important source of funds with which to purchase health insurance or make direct payments for medical expenses not covered by Medicare during retirement.

4.
Solving America's Health Care Problems through Patient Power

In general, the vision of the health care system that we accept determines what we think is possible and desirable, what we consider problems, how we analyze those problems, and how we propose to solve them.

In the cost-plus vision, which has dominated thinking about health care in the United States since the end of World War II, the primary relationships are between bureaucracies rather than between individual patients and physicians. People who accept this vision inevitably attempt to solve health care problems through bureaucratic rule making or by changing the ways in which bureaucracies relate to each other. The other vision we call Patient Power, a system under which problems would be solved by empowering individual patients and unleashing the power of competitive markets.

Ten Major Social Problems and Their Solutions

We now turn to 10 major social problems that are said to exist in the U.S. health care system and see how the competing visions of a health care system would deal with them.

1. Rising Health Care Costs

The rate of increase in America's health care spending is a serious social problem. Over the past two decades, that rate has been twice the rate of increase of the gross national product (GNP). If that trend continues, we could be spending our entire GNP on health care by the year 2062 (see

Figure 4.1

TRENDS IN HEALTH CARE SPENDING AND GNP

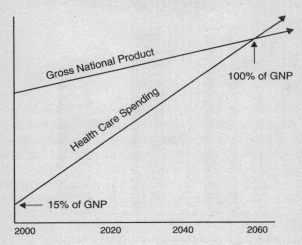

Gross National Product

100% of GNP

Health Care Spending

15% of GNP

2000   2020   2040   2060

Figure 4.1).[1]

The major reason costs are rising is that when patients and physicians get together, they are spending someone else's money rather than their own. In the hospital sector today, 95 percent of expenses are paid for by someone other than the patient, and as Figure 4.2 shows, since 1965 there has been a dramatic increase in the share of medical bills paid by third parties for every category of medical services. The share of physicians' fees paid by third parties, for example, has more than doubled, rising from 38.4 percent in 1965 to 81.3 percent in 1990. Moreover, the numbers in Figure 4.2 are averages; for many people, the extent of health insurance coverage is much greater.

One consequence of the rise in third-party payment of medical bills is that most people have no idea how much

[1] Projection based on data from the Health Care Financing Administration, Office of the Actuary.

Figure 4.2
PERCENTAGE OF PERSONAL HEALTH EXPENSES PAID BY
THIRD PARTIES, 1965 AND 1990

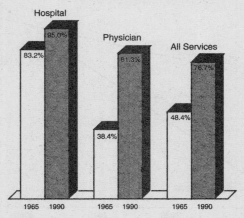

SOURCE: Health Care Financing Administration, Office of the Actuary.

they are personally contributing to cover the nation's health care costs. As Table 4.1 shows, in 1992 we spent about 12.9 percent of our GNP on health care, an amount equal to $8,000 for every U.S. household. That $8,000 burden is largely disguised, however. For a working-age family, the visible outlays are $1,580 for out-of-pocket expenses and $590 for payment for employer-provided health insurance. For the nation as a whole, such visible expenses amount to only 3.4 percent of GNP. Because the remainder of the $8,000 burden is hidden in taxes and reduced wages, there is a universal illusion that health care costs are being paid by someone else.

A related illusion is that most people cannot afford to pay for health care. In fact, they are already affording it. As Table 4.1 shows, 12.9 percent of GNP is equal to almost 20 percent of the average household's money income. Most families probably would claim that they could not possibly

Table 4.1
How We Pay for Health Care[1]

Method of Payment	Average per Household[2]	Percent of GNP	Percent of Personal Income	Percent of Money Income
Paid indirectly				
Medicare payroll taxes	$ 860	1.4%	1.6%	2.1%
Other federal, state, and local taxes[3]	3,070	4.9	5.8	7.4
Reduced wages—(employer-provided insurance)[4]	1,580	2.5	3.0	3.8
Other[5]	190	0.3	0.4	0.5
Paid directly				
Private health insurance premiums[6]	590	0.9	1.1	1.4
Out-of-pocket payments	1,580	2.5	3.0	3.8
Medicare premiums	130	0.2	0.2	0.3
Total	$8,000	12.9%	15.1%	19.4%

SOURCE: C. Eugene Steuerle, "Finance-Based Reform: The Search for an Adaptable Health Policy," Paper presented at an American Enterprise Institute conference, American Health Policy, Washington, October 3-4, 1991.

NOTE: Columns may not add to totals due to rounding.

[1] Based on estimated total health care spending for fiscal year 1992. Estimates are based on mean GNP per household of $62,160; mean personal income per household of $53,130; and mean money income per household of $41,320.

[2] Average household size in the United States was 2.63 persons in 1990. Amounts rounded to nearest $10.

[3] Includes taxes needed to finance direct government health spending out of general revenues, plus the amount that general taxes must be raised to compensate for revenue lost owing to special tax treatment of certain health-related income (about 26% of total).

[4] Employer contributions for health insurance, less government tax subsidies.

[5] Nonpatient revenue for the health care industry, including charitable donations, interest income, hospital parking, and gift shops.

[6] Includes employee contributions to private group health insurance plans, as well as individual policy premiums.

spend 20 percent of their income on health care. They would be shocked to learn that they are already spending that much.

How much should we as a nation spend on health care? Many people believe that health care spending should be determined by medical needs. Yet if we followed the practice of spending health care dollars whenever a need was being met (or a medical benefit created), we could easily spend our entire GNP on health care. In fact, we could probably spend half of the entire GNP on diagnostic tests alone. Medical science has identified at least 900 tests that can be done on blood. Except for the inconvenience, why not make all 900 part of our annual checkups? Similarly, an annual checkup could include a brain scan, a full body scan, and numerous other tests.

As an example of how the demand for the services of primary care physicians could soar, consider the trade-off between the self-administration of nonprescription drugs and the use of physicians' services. In any given year, there are about 472 million office visits to primary care physicians. But economist Simon Rottenberg estimates that, if only 2 percent of nonprescription drug consumers chose professional care rather than self-medication, the number of patient visits would climb to 721 million, thereby requiring a 50 percent increase in the number of primary care physicians. If every user of nonprescription drugs sought professional care instead, we would need 25 times the current number of primary care physicians.[2]

More diagnostic tests and increased physicians' visits are just the beginning. Once we discover something really wrong, there is almost no limit to what medical science will eventually be able to do. We are reaching a point where we can replace virtually every joint and organ, including hips, elbows, heart, and lungs, and even eyes and ears. And, like

[2] Simon Rottenberg, "Unintended Consequences: The Probable Effects of Mandated Medical Insurance," *Regulation* 13, no. 2 (Summer 1990): 27-28.

those of the bionic man, the replacements are often better than the originals. If someone else pays the bill, our potential demand for medical care could consume many times the nation's GNP, even today.

Proposals in the Cost-Plus Health Care System. From the bureaucratic perspective, some of the most commonly proposed solutions are to pass laws regulating hospital prices; to pass laws limiting the number of hospital beds and the amount of hospital equipment; to implement full-scale health care rationing; and to nationalize the entire health care system and turn the problems over to the government. Each of those solutions would widen the gap between institutional rule making and the day-to-day practice of medicine. Far from eliminating perverse incentives, they would create even more. Individuals in the medical marketplace would still find it in their self-interest to spend other people's money while bureaucracies would attempt to block the pursuit of self-interest with more rules and regulations. The government-run health care systems of other countries are not more efficient than our own, and the governments in most of those countries are attempting to keep spending down by limiting hospital budgets. That usually means denying people medical care.

Solutions through Patient Power. Health care costs cannot be controlled unless we empower individuals and make it in their self-interest to become prudent buyers of health care. When individuals have control of their own health care dollars through medical savings accounts, they won't buy unless the services are worth the price. Most of us have no idea what percentage of GNP is spent on orange juice or shoes. Because the people buying those products are spending their own money, not ours, we have no reason to care. In general, there is no right amount of money to spend on health care. The right amount is whatever people choose to spend, providing they are spending their own money and are facing prices that reflect the real social costs of medical services.

Controlling health care costs also means creating new incentives for the suppliers of services. In a competitive medical marketplace, suppliers would find it in their self-interest to lower price and improve quality and to communicate with potential buyers about price and quality.

2. The Rising Number of People Who Lack Health Insurance

In addition to the uninsurable, there is a much larger number of people who could buy insurance but choose not to. The 34.4 million Americans that some people estimate are not covered by either private or public insurance represent about 16 percent of the population. Interestingly, 85 percent of the uninsured are members of a family with a working adult; and more than half of them live in families with an adult who has steady, full-time employment.[3]

There is considerable debate over the dimensions of this problem and how much difference it makes. For example, although as much as 16 percent of the population are uninsured at any point in time, only 15 percent of those people are uninsured for two years or more.[4] Thus, being uninsured is similar to being unemployed. Although many people may experience being uninsured over the course of their work lives, only a small number experience it for a long time. Still, it is a problem that is exacerbated by unwise govern-

[3] Jill D. Foley, *Uninsured in the United States: The Nonelderly Population without Health Insurance* (Washington: Employee Benefit Research Institute, April 1991). These estimates are based on the March 1990 Current Population Survey and differ somewhat from other estimates. For example, the actual number of uninsured may be closer to 30 million people—about 12.4 percent of the population—and the proportion of uninsured with a workforce affiliation may be only 65 percent, rather than 85 percent. See the summary of the literature in Michael A. Morrisey, "Health Care Reform: A Review of Five Generic Proposals," Paper presented at Winners and Losers in Reforming the U.S. Health Care System, a policy forum sponsored by the Employee Benefit Research Institute Education and Research Fund, Washington, October 4, 1990.

[4] Katherine Swartz and Timothy D. McBride, "Spells without Health Insurance: Distributions of Durations and Their Link to Point-in-Time Estimates of the Uninsured," *Inquiry* 27 (Fall 1990).

Table 4.2
PEOPLE WITHOUT HEALTH INSURANCE, BY FAMILY INCOME LEVEL, 1989

Family Income	Number of People (Millions)
Under $5,000	4.7
$5,000-$9,999	5.0
$10,000-$14,999	5.6
$15,000-$19,999	4.6
$20,000-$29,999	5.9
$30,000-$39,999	3.2
$40,000-$49,999	1.9
$50,000 or more	3.3
Total	34.4

SOURCE: Jill D. Foley, *Uninsured in the United States: The Nonelderly Population without Health Insurance* (Washington: Employee Benefit Research Institute, April 1991), Table 5, p. 25.
NOTE: Does not add to total due to rounding.

ment policies.[5]

We have already identified three reasons for this problem. First, state legislatures keep passing regulations that increase the price of health insurance. As many as one of four uninsured people may have chosen not to purchase health insurance because of the price-increasing effects of state regulations. Second, people not covered by employer-provided health insurance are discriminated against under tax law. Unlike employees of large companies, they must pay health insurance premiums with aftertax dollars, effectively doubling the cost for many of them. Third, tax law and employee benefits law are causing employers to act in ways that result in even more employees and their dependents going without health insurance. As Table 4.2 shows, those

[5] Just as it is easy to minimize the problem, it is also easy to exaggerate it. The figure of 37 million uninsured Americans, widely reported by the national news media, includes people who lacked health insurance for brief periods (rather than continuously) during a 28-month sample period examined by the U.S. Bureau of the Census. See Spencer Rich, "28% in U.S. Seen Lacking Steady Health Insurance," *Washington Post*, April 12, 1990.

policies have the greatest impact on low-income families.

Even if they are not priced out of the market by bad public policies, many uninsured people conclude there is no reason to buy health insurance. If they get sick, they find ways of becoming insured through an employer's plan. Even if they cannot get insurance, they still get medical care—paid for by someone else.

Proposals in the Cost-Plus Health Care System. Some commonly discussed proposals are to force everyone to purchase health insurance, force employers to purchase insurance on behalf of all their employees, expand the number of people covered by Medicaid and state risk pools, and force everyone to participate in a system of national health insurance. Each of those proposals, though, ignores the principal reason why people lack health insurance in the first place: they are denied the opportunity to buy it at actuarially fair prices with equal advantage under federal tax law. Instead of encouraging market competition and giving individuals more control over their health care dollars, the proposals would force people to buy into a defective system of third-party insurance coverage and undermine the development of a genuine health insurance market.

Solutions through Patient Power. In a health care system based on Patient Power, people would face fair prices for insurance, sold in a freely competitive market. Special-interest politics would not artificially inflate health insurance premiums. All people would receive the same tax advantage for the purchase of insurance, regardless of employment. And people would have stronger incentives to purchase health insurance before they developed chronic illnesses. The Patient Power system would not ignore the fact that health insurance premiums may be beyond the means of some families. But the solution is to empower the families, not impersonal third-party bureaucracies. Through a system of tax credits, low-income families would be encouraged to exercise free choice as buyers in a health insurance marketplace.

3. Health Care Rationing

Because we could in principle spend many times our gross national product on health care, it must be rationed in some way. The primary way in which it is rationed in the United States is by individual choice. When the expected cost of medical care exceeds its expected benefit, people forgo it. For example, some people choose self-medication with nonprescription drugs. What deters them from going to the doctor's office every time is the physician's fee, the time cost, the travel cost, lost wages, and other inconveniences. As discussed earlier, if everyone who purchased nonprescription drugs saw a physician instead, the United States would need 25 times the current number of physicians.

For years advocates of socialized medicine have argued that all health care (all health care) should be free at the point of consumption and that it is unfair (and perhaps also unwise) to ask people to compare the value of health care with the cost of getting it. But if health care were made absolutely costless, the system that provides it would collapse into chaos. Thus, even in countries such as Britain and Canada where health care is theoretically free, people are deterred by other costs (including waiting costs) and an enormous amount of self-rationing goes on.

The alternative to self-rationing is bureaucratic rationing. For example, many large companies are seeking ways to deter health care spending. Most are opting for bureaucratic solutions. But at least one company, Hewlett Packard, has announced a plan that explicitly calls for employee rationing by choice. The plan involves many of the concepts discussed in this book, including giving patients more information, encouraging choices between money and medical care, and using physicians as "patient advisers rather than technicians or deliverers of care."[6] Until recently, rationing by bureauc-

---

[6] Karl Palzer, "Rationing by Choice," *Business and Health*, October 1990, pp. 60-64.

racy in the private sector was rare, confined largely to organ transplants and occasional triage situations in hospitals. Rationing is more frequent in the public sector and is increasing in the Medicare and Medicaid programs. Outside the United States, every country that has national health insurance rations health care through bureaucracies. It is almost never done through open, rational debate. Instead, politicians limit the budgets of hospitals or of area health authorities and leave rationing decisions to the health care bureaucracy. Indeed, politicians almost never admit that they are in any way responsible for rationing.

Among the characteristics of health care rationing as practiced in other developed countries are the following. If health care is rationed by bureaucracies, the tendency is to discriminate in favor of higher income patients, in favor of whites (especially male whites), and in favor of the young. The sophisticated, the wealthy, and the powerful almost always find their way to the head of rationing lines. Whereas markets empower individuals, bureaucracies empower special interests.

Rationing decisions in the United States appear to be no different. Studies have discovered that, when transplants are rationed, bureaucracies appear to discriminate on the basis of income, race, and sex. For example, a study by the Urban Institute found that, for black and white males, the higher their income, the more likely they are to receive an organ transplant.[7] In 1988, according to the United Network for Organ Sharing, whites received 97.6 percent of the pancreases and high percentages of livers, kidneys, and hearts; and men received 79.2 percent of hearts, 60.6 percent of kidneys,

---

[7] Phillip J. Held et al., "Access to Kidney Transplantation: Has the United States Eliminated Income and Racial Differences?" *Archives of Internal Medicine* 14 (December 1988): 2594-2600. A likely reason for the discrepancy is Medicare reimbursement policies, which place greater burdens on lower income patients. Prior to 1987, Medicare did not pay for outpatient drugs such as cyclosporine, which can cost transplant patients up to $5,000 per year. It would be irrational to spend $50,000 on a transplant and have it rejected because the patient could not afford $5,000 in immunosuppressive drugs for one year.

and 54.4 percent of pancreases.[8] According to the American Society of Transplant Physicians, although the rate of end-stage renal disease is four times higher among blacks than among whites, blacks constitute 28 percent of the kidney patients and receive only 21 percent of the kidney transplants.[9] *The Pittsburgh Press* found that if the donors were not living relatives, the average wait for a kidney transplant in 1988 and 1989 was 14 months for black patients and only 8.8 months for whites.[10]

In the United States, the elderly have a privileged position with respect to health care. Medicare covers virtually all of them, plus a small percentage of people under 65 (the disabled). But in other countries, where the entire population is part of the same government-funded health care plan, the elderly are usually pushed to the end of the rationing lines. Thus, in Britain, it is extremely difficult for an elderly patient to get kidney dialysis or a kidney transplant—or any other transplant, for that matter.[11] Moreover, pressures that have developed in other countries are developing in our own. Former Colorado governor Richard Lamm and other prominent individuals (including "medical ethicists") are calling for rationing health care to the elderly and reallocating the funds to the younger population.[12]

Proposals in the Cost-Plus Health Care System. Until a

[8] Associated Press, May 20, 1989.

[9] Bertram L. Kasiske, John F. Neylan III, et al., "The Effect of Race on Access and Outcome in Transplantation," *New England Journal of Medicine* 324, no. 5 (January 31, 1991): 302-7.

[10] Reported in the *Dallas Morning News,* August 19, 1990.

[11] See John C. Goodman and Gerald L. Musgrave, *Health Care for the Elderly: The Nightmare in Our Future,* NCPA Policy Report no. 130 (Dallas: National Center for Policy Analysis, October 1987); and Henry J. Aaron and William B. Schwartz, *The Painful Prescription: Rationing Hospital Care* (Washington: Brookings Institution, 1984).

[12] For a summary of these views, see Norman G. Levinsky, "Age as a criterion for Rationing Health Care," *New England Journal of Medicine* 322, no. 25 (June 21, 1990): 1813-15.

few years ago, the practitioners and defenders of cost-plus medicine did not believe in health care rationing. Their goal was to lower all financial barriers through public and private insurance and to meet any and all needs. Today, almost everyone recognizes that rationing is necessary. Many people in the modern cost-plus bureaucracy not only accept rationing but welcome it with open arms—provided, of course, that it is controlled by the (health care) bureaucracy and not by individual patients.

Solutions through Patient Power. In a Patient Power system, rationing would be by patient choice wherever possible. The system would be organized so that people would have the funds necessary to purchase health care through medical savings and reimbursements from insurers. But people would have strong incentives not to purchase health care unless the expected value of the care were greater than the monetary costs. Patients, of course, could consult their physicians. But the power of choice would be in the hands of the patients, not the bureaucrats.

4. Administrative Costs

In 1987, according to one study, each doctor in the United States spent an average of more than 134 hours filling out insurance forms. Overall, the cost of administering the U.S. health care system was estimated to be between $96.8 billion and $120.4 billion, or almost one-fourth of total health care spending that year. By contrast, the administrative costs of the Canadian system of national health insurance were estimated to be less than one-half that high.[13] Such comparisons of the administrative costs in the United States and Canada

[13] Steffie Woolhandler and David U. Himmelstein, "The Deteriorating Administrative Efficiency of the U.S. Health Care System," *New England Journal of Medicine* 324, no. 18 (May 2, 1991): 1253-58. Woolhandler and Himmelstein estimated that administrative costs as a percentage of total costs are between 8.4 percent and 11.1 percent in Canada and between 19.3 percent and 24.1 percent in the United States.

are seriously flawed. They overestimate U.S. administrative costs and underestimate Canada's. Moreover, those who assume that the United States could substantially lower its health care costs by adopting the Canadian system are engaged in wishful thinking. Countries with national health insurance try to control health care costs by limiting the amount of money that physicians and hospitals have to spend and by forcing them to ration health care. They often do so with very little oversight.

The United States, by contrast, is moving in the opposite direction. Physicians and hospital administrators spend an enormous amount of time on paperwork, not just to facilitate the exchange of money but because third-party payers also want to ensure that the medical care is appropriate and necessary. Were the United States to adopt a program of national health insurance, there is every reason to suppose that administrative costs would go up, not down. There is little chance that we would follow the Canadian practice of giving providers a fixed budget from which to ration health care with few questions asked. Nevertheless, almost everyone familiar with the administrative burdens faced by providers has concluded that the burdens are way too heavy, causing inefficiency and waste.

Proposals in the Cost-Plus Health Care System. Because the cost-plus mentality sees no value in, and no role for, a market in health care, monopoly and central planning are almost always preferred to competition and decentralization. The concept of patients' shopping in the medical marketplace and negotiating and bargaining with providers is foreign to the cost-plus way of thinking. Thus, advocates of the cost-plus system reason that if a single payer (read government) wrote all of the checks, costs would be lower than they are when the checks are written by Medicare, Medicaid, and thousands of employers and private insurers.

Solutions through Patient Power. One of the reasons

Figure 4.3
TOTAL ANNUAL HEALTH CARE COSTS PER EMPLOYEE,
1985 TO 1991

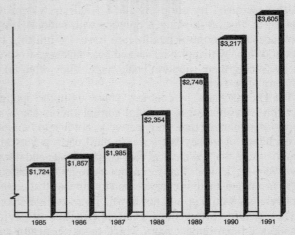

SOURCE: A. Foster Higgins & Co., *Health Care Benefits Survey, 1991: Indemnity Plans: Cost, Design and Funding.*

why administrative costs are high is precisely because the U.S health care system is bureaucratic, rather than market-based. By contrast, one of the most important functions of competitive markets is to eliminate waste and inefficiency. More than half of the money now spent by third-party payers could instead be spent by patients out of personal medical savings accounts. If those expenditures were made with health care debit cards, the administrative costs would be a little over 1 percent. Not only would there be huge savings in administrative costs, there would also be a substantial reduction in spending on unnecessary care, or care of marginal value. Overall, we estimate that if every family in America had a medical savings account covering the first $2,500 of annual medical bills, the nation's total health care spending would be reduced by as much as one-fourth, with no detrimental effect on the health of patients.

5. Controlling Costs in Employer-Provided Health Insurance Plans

As Figure 4.3 shows, between 1985 and 1991, the amount that employers spent annually on health care for each employee (and dependents) climbed from $1,724 to $3,605, an increase of 100 percent in just six years.[14] As Figure 4.4 shows, health care costs for employers have been increasing at about three times the rate of inflation, and in recent years we have witnessed double-digit increases. Even the most profitable corporations cannot sustain increases in that range for long. It would be a mistake, however, to conclude that those costs are ultimately borne by firms. Health insurance is a fringe benefit that substitutes for wages. Ultimately, therefore, the cost of wasteful health insurance comes out of the pockets of workers, not their employers.

Proposals in the Cost-Plus Health Care System. For those who seek bureaucratic solutions, the proposals run the gamut: for example, make special deals with certain hospitals and require all employees to use only those hospitals, negotiate similar contracts with selected physicians, eliminate benefits from the company's health insurance policy, require corporate approval prior to major surgery, and so forth. Each of those proposals, however, further intrudes on the doctor/patient relationship. And each new set of rules expands the system's perverse incentives. Those solutions operate within a framework in which the self-interest of employees and their physicians is diametrically opposed to the goals of the employer or the health insurance carrier, or both. To appreciate the impact of the dichotomy, consider that two-thirds of the physicians in a 1989 poll indicated a willingness to help patients get health insurance benefits by

[14] A. Foster Higgins & Co., *Health Care Benefits Survey, 1990: Indemnity Plans: Cost, Design and Funding.*

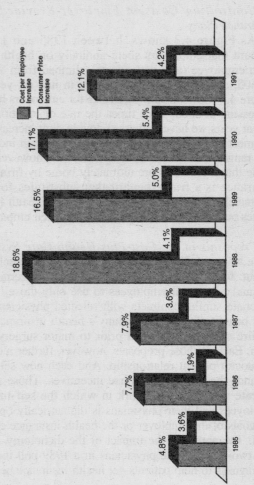

Figure 4.4

ANNUAL PERCENTAGE INCREASE IN HEALTH CARE COSTS PER EMPLOYEE, 1985 TO 1991

SOURCE: A. Foster Higgins & Co., *Health Care Benefits Survey, 1991: Indemnity Plans: Cost, Design and Funding;* and U.S. Bureau of Labor Statistics.

misrepresenting a test as being "diagnostic" rather than for "general screening."[15]

Solutions through Patient Power. If health insurance were individualized, and if employee patients controlled their own health care dollars, there would no longer be a corporate problem. The role of the employer would be to help negotiate good deals for employees or to help them choose a policy wisely. Each employee would choose a package of benefits tailored to individual and family needs. Cost-control devices, if needed, would be chosen voluntarily, not imposed from above. Moreover, for each individual employee, health insurance premiums would become a dollar-for-dollar substitute for wages. In the ideal health care system, employers would not attempt to force employees to do what was not in their self-interest in the medical marketplace. The only relevant goals would be employee goals, and the role of the employer would be to help employees reach those goals.

6. Health Insurance for Small Business

Health insurance has increasingly become prepayment for the consumption of medical care rather than genuine insurance, and the consequences have been especially detrimental for small business.

For large companies, the evolution of the prepayment concept means that each year's premiums are determined by last year's costs. Employers pay in health insurance premiums an amount equal to the cost of whatever their employees consume. That is one of the reasons why so many large employers self-insure, sometimes using insurance companies to administer their plans. In a sense, self-insurance merely formalizes a relationship that was previously implicit between the employer and the health insurance company. Moreover, because large employers have many employees,

---

[15]John C. Pezullo et al., "Physicians' Attitudes towards Using Deception to Resolve Difficult Ethical Problems," *Journal of the American Medical Association* 261, no. 20 (May 26, 1989): 2980-85.

they have a self-contained insurance pool, and their total costs are reasonably predictable.

Insurance as prepayment for the consumption of medical care has wreaked havoc among small employers, however. The principal reason why small businesses purchase health insurance is to avoid the risk of having to pay unexpectedly large medical bills. However, because the policies they purchase are not real insurance, when a small company generates a large claim, the insurer may triple or quadruple the company's premiums and may even cancel the policy. Thus, employers who thought they were buying insurance are surprised to find out that there is very little risk sharing and, instead, they are mainly expected to pay their own way.

Before turning to solutions, it is worth contrasting small group insurance with the market for individual and family policies—about the only market where real insurance is still sold. In most states, insurers cannot raise an individual's premium without raising all other premiums (for the same type of policy) by an equal amount. Thus, insurers can't single out those who get sick and charge them more than others. Moreover, the more they raise the premiums for all policyholders, the greater the risk that healthy ones will leave the pool and buy a low-priced policy from some other insurer. Problems in the market for small groups are now stimulating reform movements in almost every state, but some reforms will only make the problem worse.

Proposals in the Cost-Plus Health Care System. One of the reasons why the cost-plus system evolved was to prevent the development of a competitive health insurance market. In the 1950s, advocates of cost-plus medical care favored "community rating," a system under which everyone paid the same premium, regardless of age, sex, occupation, or any other indicator of health care risk. Such a system was bound to fail. If everyone is charged the same premium, it will be too high for healthy (low-risk) people and too low for less healthy (high-risk) people. As fewer healthy people buy health insurance, the premium needed to cover the health care costs of those who do buy will rise in a continuous upward spiral.

Today, the intellectual heirs of the architects of the cost-plus system favor a return to community rating, in either a pure or a modified form. Central to all their reform proposals is the notion that insurers should be forced to sell to anyone who wants to buy ("guaranteed issue") at prices that do not reflect real risks. Of course, the modern versions of community rating face the same problems as the older version. That is why the modern advocates also often favor employer or individual mandates, which would force people to buy health insurance whether they want to or not. The ultimate reform along those lines is national health insurance, a system under which everyone is forced to pay a tax (price) that is also unrelated to real insurance risks.

Solutions through Patient Power. To the cost-plus mentality, the purpose of health insurance is to pay medical bills. By contrast, under the Patient Power system, the purpose of health insurance would be similar to the purpose of any other type of insurance—to allow people to protect their assets by transferring risk to others. Accordingly, a Patient Power system would place a high value on pricing risk accurately and encouraging a competitive market that would accomplish that task. As in the case of life insurance, however, once people have purchased a policy, insurers should not be able to change the rules of the game simply because an individual's probability of filing a claim suddenly increases.

Many of the problems in the market for small groups would disappear if small group insurance functioned in the same way as individual insurance does. One way of moving in that direction is to individualize employer-provided health insurance. Many of the problems in the market for individual insurance would disappear if health insurance more closely resembled life insurance.

7. Preventive Medicine

Many medical procedures can potentially save lives and, possibly, money. They include chest x-rays, mammograms, pap smears, and cholesterol tests. Between 1980 and 1986, according to a study in the *International Journal of Epidemiology*, there were 121,560 deaths from disorders that are not usually lethal if discovered and treated early. They included deaths from appendicitis, pneumonia, gallbladder infection, hypertensive heart disease, asthma, and cervical cancer.[16] About 80 percent of the premature deaths reported in the study were among blacks, even though blacks make up only 13 percent of the U.S. population.

If we knew in advance which patients had serious problems, solutions would be relatively easy. But often we don't know. As a result, there is considerable debate over how many people should be tested and how frequently. One thing we do know, however, is that some people who should realize they have a problem fail either to see a physician or to receive the necessary preventive care.

The problem is especially acute in low-income areas, where there are sometimes epidemics of diseases many people thought had been eradicated only a few years ago. Some inner cities now report skyrocketing rates of tuberculosis, hepatitis A, syphilis, gonorrhea, measles, mumps, and whooping cough. All too often, those who are infected see physicians too late. For example, at Harlem Hospital in New York City, only 30 percent of the women diagnosed with breast cancer live as long as five years, compared with 70 percent of white women and 60 percent of black women in the country as a whole.[17]

Such statistics have led many to conclude that America's

[16] Eugene Schwartz, Vincent Y. Kofie, et al., "Black/White Comparisons of Deaths Preventable by Medical Intervention: United States and the District of Columbia 1980-1986," *International Journal of Epidemiology* 19, no. 3 (September 1990): 592.

[17] Elizabeth Rosenthal, "Health Problems of Inner City Poor Reach Crisis Point," *New York Times*, December 24, 1990.

private health care system is not serving low-income people and that a public system is needed. That view overlooks the fact that many of the people who are apparently not receiving needed preventive care are already part of a free public system, partly supported by funds collected from low-income, minority taxpayers. New York City, for example, is experiencing an epidemic of congenital syphilis (with about half the cases in the country), a surprising increase in cases of measles, and increasing instances of other preventable diseases.[18] Yet the city has perhaps the most extensive system of free health care and free public hospitals in the country.

In addition to low-income families (that presumably face financial constraints), many nonpoor families that can afford to purchase preventive care choose not to do so. One reason may be that diagnostic tests themselves expose patients to risks. According to one study, from 5,000 to 10,000 cases of breast cancer each year may be caused by x-rays.[19] Health insurance companies, which clearly have a direct financial interest in such questions, generally do not require or encourage preventive medical tests. But the perspective of insurers may not be the best guide. Since people frequently switch carriers, insurers have less financial interest in the long-run consequences of a failure to detect a medical problem. And paying for diagnostic tests through insurers often doubles the cost of the tests.

Moreover, carefully conducted economic studies do not confirm that preventive medicine pays for itself. With the exception of targeted high-risk groups, preventive medicine generally adds to the cost of health. It is an investment in future good health, not a cost-control device.[20] Further, atti-

---

[18] Ibid.

[19] Michael Swift, Daphne Morrell, et al., "Incidence of Cancer in 161 Families Affected by Ataxia-Telangiectasia," *New England Journal of Medicine* 325, no. 26 (December 26, 1991): 1831-36.

[20] See Louise B. Russell, *Is Prevention Better Than Cure?* (Washington: Brookings Institution, 1986).

tudes toward risk vary. Risk-averse people place a higher value on preventive medicine than do those who are less risk averse. Yet in the current health care system, the delivery of preventive medical services tends to be determined by bureaucratic reimbursement policies rather than patients' preferences.

Proposals in the Cost-Plus Health Care System. Commonly proposed solutions are to force private insurers to cover diagnostic tests (with no out-of-pocket cost to the patient), change Medicare rules to achieve the same objective for elderly patients, and make diagnostic tests free to targeted groups through a limited national health insurance program. Each of these proposals would use health insurance as a vehicle for the prepayment of the consumption of medical services. They would probably double the cost of the services. And they would give all decisionmaking power to third-party payers.

Solutions through Patient Power. An ideal health care system would recognize that the answer to the question of whether a test is worth its cost depends as much on patient preferences and attitudes toward risk as on cost-benefit calculations. In a Patient Power system, patients would be the principal buyers of health care, and test manufacturers would market directly to them, as well as to health care providers. Health insurance would not be used as wasteful prepayment for the consumption of medical care. Instead, public policy would encourage private savings for diagnostic tests.

8. People Who Are Uninsurable because They Have Preexisting Health Care Problems

A small, but not inconsequential, number of people are unable to purchase private health insurance because they have a known—usually expensive-to-treat—health problem. As Table 4.3 shows, health insurers either refuse to cover

Table 4.3

SOME HEALTH CONDITIONS THAT FREQUENTLY CAUSE HIGHER PREMIUMS, AN EXCLUSION WAIVER, OR DENIAL OF INSURANCE

Higher Premium	Exclusion Waiver	Denial
Allergies	Cataract	AIDS
Asthma	Gallstones	Ulcerative colitis
Back strain	Fibroid tumor (uterus)	Cirrhosis of liver
Hypertension (controlled)	Hernia (hiatal/inguinal)	Diabetes mellitus
Arthritis	Migraine headaches	Leukemia
Gout	Pelvic inflammatory disease	Schizophrenia
Glaucoma	Chronic otitis media (recent)	Hypertension (uncontrolled)
Obesity	Spine/back disorders	Emphysema (severe)
Psychoneurosis (mild)	Hemorrhoids	Stroke
Kidney stones	Knee impairment	Obesity
Emphysema (mild/moderate)	Asthma	Angina (severe)
Alcoholism/drug use	Allergies	Coronary artery disease
Heart murmur	Varicose veins	Epilepsy
Peptic ulcer	Sinusitis (chronic or severe)	Lupus
Colitis	Fractures	Alcoholism/drug use

SOURCE: U.S. Office of Technology Assessment, 1988.

such people or exclude them from coverage for the preexisting illness. Of course, the primary reason that people with a serious preexisting condition want health insurance is to get an insurer to pay for medical expenses they are virtually certain to incur.

A related problem occurs when people become sick while covered by one insurance carrier but then are forced to leave that carrier and search for another, either because they change jobs or because the original insurer cancels the policy. The original insurer covers the first phase of the illness, but any new insurer tries to avoid paying for its subsequent treatment. Those problems also affect other people. Large companies with health insurance plans that pay for any and all conditions, preexisting or otherwise, attract employees with medical problems, thus contributing to the companies' health insurance costs. In addition, uninsured people with such problems may generate unpaid hospital bills, which then must be paid by everyone else.

It is not surprising that private insurers refuse the obligation to pay for clearly foreseeable medical expenses. If they charged a fair premium, it would be roughly equal to the future medical expenses plus the cost of administering the policy. People with preexisting medical problems would have nothing to gain by purchasing such insurance. Still, many people face severe financial problems because they have high medical bills and no health insurance.

Before turning to solutions, it is worth asking why we do not have asimilar problem in a related field: life insurance. The answer is that most people have the opportunity to buy life insurance that is "guaranteed renewable" long before they develop a serious illness. As a result, they can continue paying premiums and can expect a large payment to their beneficiaries even if they are diagnosed with a terminal illness.

Interestingly, most individual and family health insurance policies sold in the 1950s were also guaranteed renewable. If a person became sick while covered by a health insurance policy, that person could count on indefinite coverage of medical bills. Today it's almost impossible to find a health insurance policy that is guaranteed renewable. Why? There are apparently three reasons. First, because state regulations impose onerous burdens on any insurance company that sells such policies, they have been regulated almost out of existence. Second, the tax law has encouraged the development of a health insurance system that is almost entirely employer-based, despite the increasing mobility in U.S. labor markets; when people switch jobs, they almost always have to switch health insurance policies, and the new carrier typically tries to avoid paying for preexisting illnesses. Third, government policy has encouraged health insurance to evolve into prepayment for the consumption of medical care. To a large extent, real health insurance no longer exists.

Proposals in the Cost-Plus Health Care System. The most common proposals would force insurers to cover preexisting illnesses, often with no additional premium. Many state-mandated health insurance benefit laws already attempt to do that with respect to certain health conditions. Under proposals being considered in many states, insurers would not be able to deny anyone a health insurance policy, or charge a higher premium, because of a preexisting condition. The losses that insurers incurred would be subsidized by a tax imposed on all health insurance sold in the state. Another proposal would create state risk pools that would allow patients with preexisting conditions to purchase health insurance at subsidized rates. In most states that already have risk pools, the losses are covered by taxing the health insurance premiums of everyone outside the pool.

Each of those proposals would use health insurance to prepay for the consumption of medical care. People who are already sick would pay premiums well below the actuarially fair value. The losses would be subsidized by forcing others to pay more than the actuarially fair value. In other words, the proposals would force some people to pay for the medical expenses of others. Although the objective may seem humane, the proposals are highly regressive, imposing special burdens on low-income families in order to benefit middle- and upper-income families. As is the case with existing state-mandated benefits laws (which also primarily benefit the middle class), the proposals would raise the price of insurance, thereby imposing a tax on low-income consumers or causing more of them to forgo health insurance altogether.

Solutions through Patient Power. If there is a social reason to bail out uninsured people with high medical bills, the efficient way to do so would be through direct monetary payments to those people. An income-related system of disability payments would accomplish that goal. If there is a social reason to subsidize health insurance for some, the efficient and fair way to do it would be to make the subsidy income related, giving the most help to those with the greatest need. Our recent experiences with risk pools suggest that the subsidy would not have to be that large. Currently, about 13 states have mature risk pools, which have been in operation for some period of time. In general, people with preexisting conditions are able to buy into the pool for premiums that average about 50 percent higher than comparable policies for other people. Even with the high premiums, the risk pools lose about $53 million a year. By one estimate, if that system were extended to all the states, the nationwide deficit would be about $300 million,[21] less than one-twentieth of 1 percent of the nation's annual health care bill. Under a system of public subsidies, with the subsidy falling as income rises, the taxpayer's burden would be even smaller.

In the ideal health care system, real insurance, with actuarially fair premiums, would be encouraged and promoted. Government programs to help those in need would work within the context of a competitive health insurance market, rather than undermine the market. Moreover, many of the

---

[21] Karl J. Knable, Morris Melloy, and C. Keith Powell, "State Health Insurance Risk Pools," *Health Section News*, no. 21, April 1991, pp. 9-12.

problems discussed here would never arise in an individual-ized health insurance marketplace. If health insurance were tailored to individual needs, not employer needs, it would anticipate job changes, the long-term consequences of recur-ring illness, and other problems. If health insurance were sold in a competitive marketplace, it would probably resemble life insurance. Because guaranteed renewable policies are valu-able and desirable, a market for such policies would quite likely develop.

9. Uncompensated Hospital Care

Each year American hospitals have about $8 billion in uncollected charges. It is not clear how much of that amount is unpaid because people cannot afford to pay and how much is unpaid simply because the hospitals make insufficient efforts to collect. Some studies suggest that half of uncol-lected hospital bills are generated by patients who have health insurance coverage.[22]

Almost all businesses have some bad debts. But con-sumers seldom have reason to care. In the health care system, things are different. Third-party payers pay not only for the medical care of their policyholders but also for the bad debts of others. In other words, the hospital rates that you and I pay are partly determined by how many other patients fail to pay. Bad debts are not distributed evenly among the nation's hos-pitals. For example, a special problem arises for hospitals des-ignated to receive charity patients. In many communities, those hospitals are county hospitals. County hospitals com-plain that they are undercompensated from public funds for the care they provide. They also complain of patient dump-ing—the practice of transferring charity patients from other hospitals to county hospitals, in some cases risking the health

[22] See Robert M. Saywell et al., "Hospital and Patient Characteristics of Uncompensated Hospital Care: Policy Implications," *Journal of Health Politics, Policy and Law* 14, no. 2 (Summer 1989): 287; and Congressional Research Service, *Costs and Effects of Extending Health Insurance Coverage* (Washington: October 1988), pp. 101, 103.

of the patient.[23]

Proposals in the Cost-Plus Health Care System. The most common proposals are similar to those for dealing with the uninsured. They would force all people to have health insurance, either through their place of employment or through national health insurance. Those proposals could cost in excess of $100 billion, while reducing hospital bad debts by only about $8 billion.

Solutions through Patient Power. In a Patient Power system, hospitals would be expected to cover their costs while charging competitive prices to all patients. Some provision would exist to reimburse hospitals for indigent care under carefully defined conditions. When those conditions were met, the best solution would be to reimburse hospitals from public funds rather than to attempt to shift the cost of care to other patients. If hospitals are required by law to treat patients, whether or not the patients can pay, then the government (and voter-taxpayers) imposing that requirement should be willing to pay the cost. That provision should not relieve hospitals of the responsibility of collecting fees, however. Those with excessive bad debts would be allowed to fail.

In a Patient Power system, people would be encouraged to insure for major illnesses and save for minor ones. But no one would be forced to do so. People who failed to purchase health insurance and incurred bad hospital debts would suffer financial penalties, the same as for other bad debts.

10. Long-Term Nursing Home Care for the Elderly
Currently, Medicare does not pay for long-term nursing home care for elderly patients. Medicaid (for the poor) will pay, but only after an elderly patient has exhausted virtually all personal financial resources. One consequence is that nurs-

---

[23] See L. M. Beitsch, "Economic Patient Dumping: Whose Life Is It Anyway?" *Journal of Legal Medicine* 10, no. 3 (1989): 433-87; and "Dumping Mandated by Law," *AAPS News* 47, no. 1 (January 1991).

ing home care is the largest single health care expense likely to confront an elderly individual. As Figure 4.5 shows, of out-of-pocket expenses for the elderly in excess of $2,000, about 81 percent goes for long-term care.

Is there a need for additional nursing home care for the elderly? That's not clear. For every elderly person in a nursing home, two other—equally disabled—elderly people are not. That situation reflects the fact that, when people are forced to pay with their own money, many find cheaper options. Nursing home care costs about $25,000 a year, in part owing to government regulations that require most nursing homes to be structurally safer than the average Hilton Hotel. For the most part, Medicaid patients in nursing homes cannot take the money spent on their behalf and try to find the same care for a lower price. As with other parts of the health care sector, the

Figure 4.5

ANNUAL OUT-OF-POCKET EXPENSES FOR THE ELDERLY IN EXCESS OF $2,000

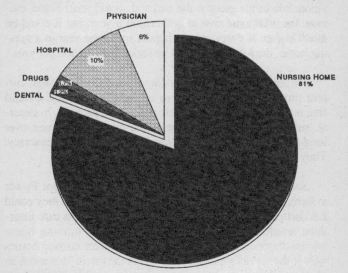

SOURCE: Health Care Financing Administration.

system is not designed to help patients find a good deal or a reasonable price. Rather, it is designed to funnel billions of dollars into nursing homes.

There is very little private insurance for nursing home care. One reason is that it is extremely difficult to construct objective definitions of the circumstance under which nursing home care is indicated. Entry into a nursing home requires a physician's statement that the treatment is necessary, but physicians often base their judgments, not on the patient's medical condition, but on family preferences. Nursing home care very often is a choice about living arrangements rather than a medical necessity. Another reason for the lack of long-term care insurance is federal tax policy, which creates tax subsidies for health insurance for current medical expenses but disallows tax deductions for premiums for future medical expenses. Savings or insurance premiums for future medical expenses must be paid with aftertax dollars.

There is no question that if nursing home care were provided free to the elderly, the demand would soar. Some estimate the additional cost at $60 billion a year, but it could be much higher. If every elderly person spent one year in a nursing home, the total cost would be about $627 billion per year.

Proposals in the Cost-Plus Health Care System. Most current proposals encourage us to ignore the costs and extend free nursing home care to elderly Medicare patients. In general, such proposals would concentrate even more power over long-term care dollars in the hands of a federal bureaucracy. They would not give the elderly more choices.

Solutions through Patient Power. Under a Patient Power system, patients would not stay in nursing homes if they could find better options at lower prices. Real long-term care insurance would make payments to people, not nursing home administrators. Individual patients would enter nursing homes only if the services offered were worth the price. Moreover, an ideal tax system would encourage savings for long-term care.

5.
Encouraging Self-Insurance through Medical Savings Accounts

The vehicle by which we spend other people's money in the medical marketplace is third-party health insurance (provided by an employer, an insurance company, or government). Prior to 1965, increases in health care costs were relatively modest because a large part of the payment was made out-of-pocket by patients. Since then, Medicare and Medicaid have expanded government third-party insurance to more and more services for the elderly and the poor, and private health insurance has expanded for the working population. As Table 5.1 shows, 95 percent of the money Americans now spend in hospitals is someone else's money

Table 5.1

SHARE OF PERSONAL HEALTH EXPENDITURES PAID BY THIRD PARTIES, 1965 AND 1990

Type of Service	1965	1990
Hospital	83.2%	95.0%
Physician	38.4	81.3
Drugs	6.4	26.4
Nursing home	35.5	55.2
All other professional services	NA	72.2
All personal health care expenditures	48.4	76.7

SOURCE: Health Care Financing Administration, Office of the Actuary. Data from the Office of National Cost Estimates.

at the time they spend it. Four-fifths of all physicians' payments are now made with other people's money, as are more than three-quarters of all medical payments for all purposes.

The expansion of third-party insurance coverage since 1965 has had a predictable consequence: health care spending has soared from 6 percent to 14 percent of our gross national product, and the rate of increase shows no sign of abating.

Numerous economic studies have shown that the amount of medicalcare that people consume varies with the out-of-pocket price they have to pay, often with no effect on health. For example, a RAND Corporation study found that people who had access to free care spent about 50 percent more than those who had to pay 95 percent of their bills out-of-pocket (up to a maximum of $1,000). People who had free care were about 25 percent more likely to see a physician and 33 percent more likely to enter a hospital.[1] Despite differences in consumption, there were no apparent differences between the two groups in terms of health outcomes. The RAND study was conducted between 1974 and 1982. A $1,000 deductible over that period would be equivalent to a deductible of between $1,380 and $2,482 today.

The Self-Insurance Alternative

People familiar with insurance have long known that it creates perverse incentives for the insured. To take advantage of the benefits under their policies, the beneficiaries do things they would not otherwisedo. In recognition of that fact, insurance in most fields is restricted to risks beyond the control of the insured. (For example, automobile casual-

---

[1] See Robert Brook et al., *The Effect of Coinsurance on the Health of Adults* (Santa Monica, Calif.: RAND Corporation, 1984); and Willard Manning et al., "Health Insurance and the Demand for Health Care: Evidence from a Randomized Experiment," *American Economic Review* 77, no. 3 (June 1987). For a survey of economic studies of the demand for medical care, see Paul Feldstein, *Healthcare Economics* (New York: John Wiley & Sons, 1988).

ty insurance does not pay for oil changes, tire rotation, brake adjustment, or other routine maintenance, even though those activities are important for the health of a car and the safety of its driver.) Financial advisers almost always recommend high-deductible policies, because low-dollar claims are the ones in which the most abuse is likely to occur so the premiums needed to cover such claims are often much too high relative to the extra coverage. The same principles apply to health insurance.

The alternative to third-party insurance is self-insurance. Rather than rely on insurers to pay every medical bill, we could put money aside in personal savings for the small expenses involved and use insurance only for rare, high-dollar medical episodes. Such a practice would result in much lower premiums and curtail a great deal of wasteful spending. But instead of exploiting opportunities for self-insurance and taking advantage of its benefits in the health care field, we have moved in the opposite direction, with insurers paying for all manner of routine expenses, including checkups and diagnostic tests, even when there is no illness and no risky event has occurred.

Why Low-Deductible Health Insurance Is Wasteful

Because employees, through their employers, are able to purchase health insurance with pretax dollars but individuals are not permitted to self-insure (personal savings) for small medical expenses with pretax dollars, people often buy low-deductible health insurance and use insurers to pay small medical bills that would be much less expensive if paid out-of-pocket. The following examples show how wasteful this practice can be.

The Cost of a Low-Deductible Policy in Cities with Average Health Care Costs

The cost of catastrophic health insurance is usually quite low. Consider a standard individual health insurance policy for a middle-aged male in a city with average health care

Table 5.2

COST OF LOWER DEDUCTIBLES FOR A 40-YEAR-OLD MAN IN A
CITY WITH AVERAGE HEALTH CARE COSTS[1]

Lowering the Deductible[2]	Additional Annual Premium	Cost of Each $1 of Additional Coverage[3]
From $2,500 to $1,000	$168.84	14¢
From $1,000 to $500	255.12	64
From $500 to $250	153.24	77

SOURCE: Golden Rule Insurance Co.

[1]Data are for 1991.

[2]For deductibles of $1,000 or less, the policy has a 20 percent copayment up to a maximum of $1,000.

[3]Because the policy has a 20 percent copayment, additional coverage is 80 percent of the difference between the two deductibles.

costs, such as Indianapolis (see Table 5.2). If the policy has a $2,500 deductible, the policyholder is at risk for $2,500. The insurance company, on the other hand, is at risk for $1 million. Given an average premium, that health insurance costs the policyholder about 6/100th of one penny in premiums for each dollar of coverage.

Now contrast that policy with a $1,000-deductible policy that has a 20 percent copayment for the next $5,000 of expenses. In theory, the $1,000 deductible gives the policyholder $1,500 of extra insurance coverage. But because of the 20 percent copayment, the additional coverage actually is only $1,200.[2] People who choose the $1,000 deductible will pay about $169 in additional premiums in return for $1,200 of additional insurance coverage. As a result, each additional dollar of insurance coverage costs the policyhold-

[2] Unless the policyholders have reached the cap on their copayment ($1,000), they must pay 20 percent of medical expenses above the deductible. Thus, if policyholders with a $1,000 deductible have medical expenses of $2,500, they must pay the first $1,000 plus 20 percent of the next $1,500 (or $300). The insurance company, in this instance, will pay $1,200.

er 14 cents.[3] Table 5.2 also shows the marginal cost (premium increase per additional dollar of coverage) of buying down the deductible even further. As the table shows, lowering the deductible from $1,000 to $500 costs 64 cents in additional premiums for each additional dollar of insurance coverage. Lowering the deductible from $500 to $250 costs 77 cents in additional premiums for each additional dollar of insurance coverage.

In general, buying a $250-deductible policy rather than a $500-deductible policy is a good deal only if the policyholder is confident he will have at least $500 in medical expenses. Even in that case, the gain is small—a dollar's worth of medical expenses for each 77 cents in premiums. For the vast majority of people, however, a low-deductible policy is quite wasteful. Considering the administrative expenses, insurers on the average will pay out only 54 cents in claims for each 77 cents in premiums. Policyholders as a group, therefore, will pay far more in premiums than they will receive in benefits.

The Cost of a Low-Deductible Policy in Cities with High Health Care Costs

In general, the higher the health care costs in an area, the more expensive low-deductible health insurance becomes. Table 5.3, for example, shows the costs of a lower deductible for a middle-aged male in a city such as Miami. As the table shows, lowering the deductible from $2,500 to $1,000 is quite expensive—33 cents for each additional dollar of coverage. Lowering the deductible from $1,000 to $500 is inherently wasteful, costing $1.79 for each additional dollar of coverage. Lowering the deductible from $500 to $250

---

[3] These calculations are based on policies sold by Golden Rule Insurance Co., the largest seller of individual and family policies in the country. Other insurance companies sell similar policies at similar prices. See John C. Goodman and Gerald L. Musgrave, *Controlling Health Care Costs with Medical Savings Accounts*, NCPA Policy Report no. 168 (Dallas: National Center for Policy Analysis, January 1992).

Table 5.3

COST OF LOWER DEDUCTIBLES FOR A 40-YEAR-OLD MAN IN A
CITY WITH HIGH HEALTH CARE COSTS[1]

Lowering the Deductible[2]	Additional Annual Premium	Cost of Each $1 of Additional Coverage[3]
From $2,500 to $1,000	$389.64	$0.33
From $1,000 to $500	715.44	1.79
From $500 to $250	440.28	2.20

SOURCE: Golden Rule Insurance Co.
[1]Data are for 1991.
[2]For deductibles of $1,000 or less, the policy has a 20 percent copayment up to a maximum of $1,000.
[3]Because the policy has a 20 percent copayment, additional coverage is 80 percent of the difference between the two deductibles.

costs $2.20 for each additional dollar of coverage, or $1.20 more than any possible benefits the policyholder could derive.

The Cost of a Low-Deductible Policy under Blue Cross Plans in California

Southern California has health care costs that are among the highest in the nation. As a result, Californians who buy lower deductible policies are being especially wasteful. Table 5.4 shows what policyholders would pay to reduce the deductible under Blue Cross plans currently sold for individuals and families in different age groups. Even lowering the deductible from $2,000 to $1,000 is a bad buy in many cases. A deductible of less than $1,000 is always a bad buy.

A California couple with no children will pay from $1.44 to $2.64 (depending on their age) for each dollar of additional insurance if they choose a $500 rather than a $1,000 deductible. If they further lower the deductible to $250, they will pay from $1.92 to $9.54 for each additional dollar of coverage.

Table 5.4

BLUE CROSS PLANS IN SOUTHERN CALIFORNIA: COST OF LOWER DEDUCTIBLES*

Status and Age	Cost per Dollar of Additional Insurance Coverage for		
	Lowering Deductible from $2,000 to $1,000	Lowering Deductible from $1,000 to $500	Lowering Deductible from $500 to $250
Single person			
Under 30	$0.14	$0.72	$1.80
30-39	0.20	1.05	1.02
40-49	0.27	1.20	1.80
50-59	0.42	0.99	2.82
60-64	0.51	1.08	3.84
Subscriber and spouse			
Under 30	$0.29	$1.44	$2.28
30-39	0.24	2.52	1.92
40-49	0.51	2.07	4.62
50-59	0.77	2.64	5.64
60-64	1.02	1.71	9.54
Subscriber and child			
Under 30	$0.15	$0.96	$1.62
30-39	0.23	1.14	1.74
40-49	0.24	1.86	2.58
50-59	0.38	2.55	3.18
60-64	0.53	1.05	5.34

(Continued on next page)

Table 5.4—Continued

BLUE CROSS PLANS IN SOUTHERN CALIFORNIA: COST OF LOWER DEDUCTIBLES*

Status and Age	Cost per Dollar of Additional Insurance Coverage for		
	Lowering Deductible from $2,000 to $1,000	Lowering Deductible from $1,000 to $500	Lowering Deductible from $500 to $250
Family			
Under 30	$0.42	$2.52	$2.22
30–39	0.56	2.16	3.60
40–49	0.62	2.82	4.68
50–59	0.87	3.90	5.04
60–64	1.16	2.04	10.14
Subscriber and children			
Under 30	$0.27	$1.38	$2.52
30–39	0.29	0.96	3.90
40–49	0.30	1.44	4.62
50–59	0.44	1.44	6.96
60–64	0.62	1.23	6.18

SOURCE: Blue Cross.
*For Orange, Santa Barbara, and Ventura counties in California in 1991.

YES! I support Patient Power, not government control of health care.

☐ Send me ____ copy(s) of this book.
   1 copy $4.95   5 copies $15.00
   50 copies $100.00   100 copies $125.00 $ _____

☐ Send me ____ copy(s) of the full-length
   (673-page) *Patient Power* at $16.95. $ _____

☐ I'd like to become a Cato Sponsor for
   $50 and receive regular reports on
   policy issues. $ _____

                     TOTAL $ _____

☐ My check payable to
   Cato Institute is enclosed.

☐ Charge my: ☐ VISA ☐ MasterCard

Account # _____

Exp. date _____

Signature _____

Name _____

Address _____

City _____ State _____ Zip _____

Figure 5.1
ANNUAL PREMIUM SAVINGS FOR A 40-YEAR-OLD MAN IF THE DEDUCTIBLE IS INCREASED FROM $250 TO $1,000*

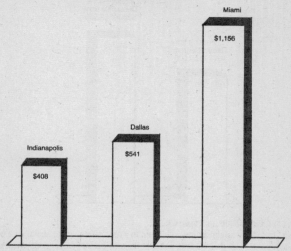

SOURCE: Golden Rule Insurance Co.

*Data are for an individual male aged 40 in 1991. Because the policy has a 20 percent copayment, the increase in the deductible eliminates only $600 of health insurance coverage unless the policyholder has medical expenses in excess of $5,000.

Opportunities for Premium Savings

Because low-deductible health insurance is so wasteful, in most places people would realize substantial premium savings if they increased the deductible. For example, the average employee in the U.S. economy has a deductible of about $250.[4] If it were increased to $1,000, the employee would lose $600 worth of coverage (80% x $750).

Figure 5.1 shows the potential annual savings on individual policies sold in Indianapolis (an average health care cost

---

[4] See John C. Goodman, Aldona Robbins, and Gary Robbins, *Mandating Health Insurance*, NCPA Policy Report no. 136 (Dallas: National Center for Policy Analysis, February 1988).

Figure 5.2
ANNUAL PREMIUM SAVINGS IF THE DEDUCTIBLE IS INCREASED FOR
FAMILIES IN CITIES WITH AVERAGE HEALTH CARE COSTS*

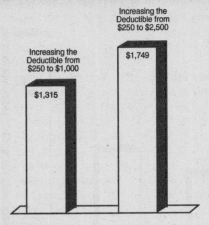

SOURCE: Golden Rule Insurance Co.
*Data are for two adults and two children in a city with average health care costs.
For deductibles less than $2,500, policyholders face a 20 percent copayment up to
$1,000. Unless policyholders have medical expenses of $5,000, they forgo $600
of coverage by moving up from a $250 deductible to a $1,000 deductible and
$1,800 of coverage by moving up from a $250 deductible to a $2,500 deductible.

city), Dallas (an above-average cost city), and Miami (a
high-cost city). As the figure shows, in return for giving up
$600 of coverage, policyholders would realize immediate
savings of 68 percent of that amount in Indianapolis and 90
percent in Dallas through lower premiums. In Miami policyholders would save $1,156 in reduced premium payments,
or $556 more than the coverage they would forgo.

In most places, the savings for families that choose higher deductibles are even greater. In a city with average health
care costs, families can save about $1,315 a year by choos-
ing a $1,000 deductible rather than a $250 deductible—savings that are more than twice as much as the value of the
coverage forgone. By choosing a $2,500 deductible rather
than a $250 deductible, they can save $1,749, or $51 less

than the value of the coverage they forgo (see Figure 5.2).[5]

However, under current federal tax law, if such policies are purchased by employers who attempt to pass the savings on to their employees in the form of higher wages, up to half the premium savings will go to the government in the form of taxes.

Opportunities for Premium Savings in Large Groups

Considerable savings are possible for individuals and families who choose higher deductible policies, for two reasons. First, when policyholders spend more of their own money on small medical bills, they are more prudent consumers; they hold down medical costs and, therefore, health insurance premiums. Second, when people have the choice between higher and lower deductibles, healthy people tend to choose high-deductible policies whereas those who are not as healthy tend to choose low deductibles. Thus, people who choose high deductibles are less of an insurance risk.

Suppose, however, that an employer with a large group of employees increased the deductible for every member of the group—the healthy as well as the sick. In that case, any reduction in total medical expenses would be attributable solely to changes in the employees' consumption behavior. But even if there were no behavior changes, health insurance premiums could be cut substantially.

Many people, including representatives of major employers and large insurance companies, question whether there are substantial savings in raising the deductible. Yet the claims experience of large groups show that substantial savings do occur. The reason for the confusion is that apparently contradictory statements can be made about the distribution of claims. For example:

- About 4 percent of the people account for 50 percent of health care spending and 20 percent of the people account for 80 percent of the spending.

[5] The forgone coverage is 80% x ($2,500 - $250) = $1,800.

Figure 5.3

DISTRIBUTION OF MEDICAL EXPENSES AMONG 50 PEOPLE*

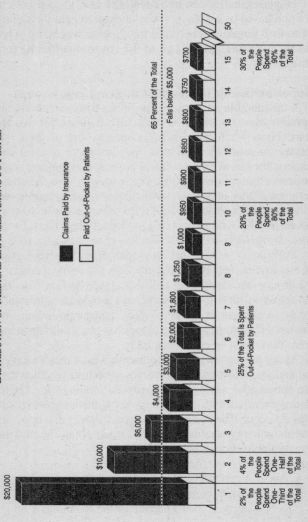

Claims Paid by Insurance
Paid Out-of-Pocket by Patients

65 Percent of the Total

Falls below $5,000

25% of the Total is Spent Out-of-Pocket by Patients

| 1 | 2 | 3 | 4 | 5 | 6 | 7 | 8 | 9 | 10 | 11 | 12 | 13 | 14 | 15 | 50 |

$20,000 $10,000 $6,000 $4,000 $3,000 $2,000 $1,800 $1,250 $1,000 $950 $900 $850 $800 $750 $700

2% of the People Spend One-Third of the Total

4% of the People Spend One-Half of the Total

20% of the People Spend 80% of the Total

30% of the People Spend 90% of the Total

*Assumes a $250 deductible and a 20 percent copayment on the next $5,000 of expenses. Period of coverage is one year.

- About two-thirds of all health care spending is on medical bills of $5,000 or less.

The first statement, popularized in a widely distributed Blue Cross-Blue Shield publication,[6] implies to many people that most of the money is spent on people who are very sick. By contrast, the second statement implies that most medical bills are small. As Figure 5.3 shows, both statements are correct. The distribution of medical expenses in Figure 5.3 is a reasonable representation of what happens in most large groups. In this case, 50 people spend $60,000, or $1,200 per person, on the average. A small percentage of people spend most of the money and at the same time two-thirds of spending is on medical bills below $5,000. If the example were broadened to include a much larger group, the extremes of the distribution would become more evident. A few people would have medical expenses of several hundred thousand dollars, and many others would have no medical claims. The characteristics of the distribution, however, would be about the same as those shown in Figure 5.3.

When individuals are given a choice, those who choose a $1,000 deductible rather than a $250 deductible can expect a one-third reduction in health insurance premiums. A one-third reduction in claims costs (and therefore in premiums)[7] is possible for a large group if the deductible is increased from $250 to about $2,500. Considering that higher deductibles cause people to change their behavior, however, a one-third reduction in premiums for a large group would probably occur at a deductible of between $1,000 and $2,500.

Winners and Losers with Higher Deductibles

Except in those instances in which people pay more in premiums than the value of coverage they receive, higher

[6] Blue Cross and Blue Shield System, *Reforming the Small Group Health Insurance Market*, March 1991, p. 6.

[7] Assumes that administrative costs are proportional to claims, an assumption that is consistent with industry experience.

deductibles represent a gamble. On the one hand, a higher deductible results in premium savings. On the other hand, it puts policyholders at greater risk. Thus, some people will gain from a higher deductible and others will lose. A priori, most people won't know which group they are in.

As Figure 5.3 shows, the vast majority of people would gain from a higher deductible. In any one year, about 70 percent would have very few medical expenses, accounting for only 2.5 percent of all health insurance claims. Those who had large medical bills, on the other hand, would be worse off. Nevertheless (as discussed below), even people who had high medical expenses in any one year would be better off with a high deductible, provided they did not have recurring large medical bills over many years. Take a leukemia patient, for example, who faces large medical expenses indefinitely. With a high annual deductible, the out-of-pocket costs for that patient will simply rise over time.

However, there are ways of structuring health insurance so that even potential leukemia patients are better off with a high deductible. Instead of the annual deductible that is common these days, health insurance could have a "per condition deductible" as was common some years ago. With a per condition deductible, a person diagnosed with cancer would pay the deductible only once, and insurance would pay all of the remaining costs of the cancer treatments, even if those costs were incurred over many years.

Allowing People to Self-Insure through Medical Savings Accounts

To help eliminate the perverse incentives in the current system, we should allow individuals to make tax-free deposits each year to personal medical savings accounts. Those accounts would serve as self-insurance and as an alternative to the wasteful use of third-party insurers for small medical bills. Funds in the accounts would grow tax-free, and withdrawals would be permitted only for legitimate medical expenses. Funds not spent during a person's working years could be spent on postretirement health care or rolled over into a pension fund.

Medical savings accounts would be the private property of the account holders and become part of an individual's estate at the time of death. If created by an employer, they would be personal and portable for the employee. Contributions to medical savings accounts should receive at least as much tax encouragement as payments for conventional health insurance.[8]

Case Study: Family Health Insurance Premiums in Indianapolis

Consider a male employee (age 35) with a dependent wife and one child living in Indianapolis. Under a conventional group health insurance policy, the premium for the family would be $3,330. The policy has a $250 per person deductible and a 20 percent copayment up to a maximum out-of-pocket expense of $1,000 per person.[9] Thus the family's exposure—the amount of potential liability—is $3,750 (three $1,000 potential copayments plus three $250 deductibles).

Now consider a policy covering identical services but with a single "umbrella" deductible of $3,000.[10] If the family chooses such a policy, its exposure actually decreases by $750 (the difference between the $3,000 deductible and the

[8] The concept of medical savings accounts, called the health bank, was originated by Jesse Hixson, currently a health policy economist with the American Medical Association. For some recent analyses of medical savings accounts, see John C. Goodman, "Personal Medical Savings Accounts (Medical IRAs): An Idea Whose Time Has Come," NCPA Policy Backgrounder no. 128, Dallas, National Center for Policy Analysis, July 22, 1993; Gerald L. Musgrave, "Emotions, Politics and Economics: An Introduction to Healthcare," *Business Economics* 28 no. 2 (1993): 7-10; and Merrill Matthews, Jr., "Medisave Accounts: The Ethical Health Reform," *Wall Street Journal,* September 16, 1993.

[9] Figures provided by Golden Rule Insurance Company.

[10] In other words, the family pays the first $3,000 of expenses, and the insurer pays all expenses above $3,000. This policy, which was developed for the small group market, is currently being test marketed by Golden Rule Insurance Company.

Figure 5.4
GROWTH OF MEDICAL SAVINGS ACCOUNTS WITH $1,605 ANNUAL DEPOSITS*

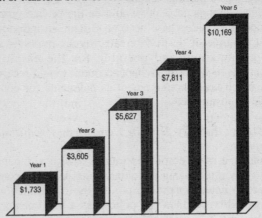

*End-of-year balance. Assumes 8 percent interest.

$3,750 of exposure under the traditional policy). However, the price of the umbrella policy is only $1,725. By purchasing the catastrophic policy, the employee and his employer not only reduce the family's total exposure, they also save the $1,605 difference in the price of the two policies.

Most people have no medical expenses in any given year, and it is not uncommon for people to go for several years without incurring medical costs. As noted above, a family in a city with average health care costs can expect to save about $1,605 in insurance premiums if it chooses a $3,000 rather than a $250 deductible. Suppose that savings were placed in a medical savings account. Figure 5.4 shows how medical savings account balances would grow over time if none of the money were spent. The family would soon have a considerable amount of money with which to pay medical expenses below the $3,000 deductible of their policy.

Encouraging Self-Insurance: A Revenue-Neutral Proposal
    One way to encourage medical savings accounts without

any loss of revenue to the federal government is to permit employers and employees to choose higher deductible policies and place the untaxed premium savings in medical savings accounts.[11] For employees, there would be no change in the amount reserved for health care benefits or in the total tax subsidy for employee benefits. And the change would encourage prudence, eliminate waste, and give employees greater control over their health care dollars.

Currently, many large employers maintain flexible spending accounts (FSAs) for their employees under section 125 of the Internal Revenue Code. Under that arrangement, employees can reduce their salaries and make contributions to an individual FSA with pretax dollars. The funds are then used to pay medical expenses at the employee's discretion. The only difference between an FSA and a medical savings account is that FSA funds are governed by a "use it or lose it" requirement. If employees fail to spend the entire amount in their FSAs in one year, they forfeit the balance.[12] Thus, the incentives created by FSAs are the opposite of those created by medical savings accounts; employees are penalized for not spending FSA funds. A small change in the tax law could change that perverse incentive into a positive incentive: "Use it or keep it."

Extending Medical Savings Accounts to Others: A Non-Revenue-Neutral Proposal

Although the federal government grants generous tax subsidies to employer-provided health insurance, a deduction of only 25 percent is given to self-employed people who purchase their own health insurance. No deduction is given for the purchase of health insurance by the unemployed,

---

[11] Under the current budget rules, any change in policy proposed in Congress must not cause a net loss of federal revenue. The forecasting techniques used to estimate revenue effects are "static" rather than "dynamic," however. Thus, forecasters tend to ignore any behavioral economic responses that would result from a change in the composition of the total amount of nontaxed employee benefits.

[12] See Alain Enthoven, "Health Policy Mismatch," *Health Affairs* (Winter 1985).

employees of firms that do not provide health insurance, or employees who must pay for health insurance coverage for their dependents with aftertax dollars.

Most of the 37 million Americans who lack health insurance have no tax encouragement to obtain it. One of the most effective ways to increase the number of people with health insurance would be to grant a tax deduction (or tax credit) to individuals who purchase health insurance with aftertax dollars.[13] Because the purchase of health insurance would remain voluntary, that would create far fewer distortions in the labor market than would mandating employer-provided insurance. At the same time we extend tax encouragement for third-party insurance to all Americans, we should also establish tax incentives to self-insure for small medical bills.[14]

Creating Medical Savings Accounts in Public Programs

Under the current system, the political pressures governing Medicare (for the elderly) and Medicaid (for the poor) are to expand benefits and to refuse to pay for them. One consequence is increasing evidence of health care rationing. Medical savings accounts could solve problems in both programs. For example, pregnant Medicaid women might have an account to draw on that they could freely spend in the medical marketplace. That would empower patients and expand the number of providers to whom they have access. Similarly, the elderly could choose higher Medicare deductibles and make deposits to their own medical savings accounts.

Advantages of Medical Savings Accounts

Creating individual and family medical savings accounts would represent a major departure from the current system

---

[13] See Goodman, Robbins, and Robbins.

[14] For example, individuals might be given a tax deduction for the amount of money that would be necessary to purchase a standard $250-deductible policy. For the purchase of higher deductible policies, taxpayers could be granted the right to deposit the premium savings in medical savings accounts.

of paying for health care. Those accounts would have immediate advantages, which would become even more important over time. The 12 principal advantages follow.

1. Preserving the American Tradition of Individual Responsibility

Nearly all other proposals for health care reform involve some form of mandate either on businesses to provide insurance or on individuals to purchase insurance.[15] Not only do such mandates violate the American tradition of individual responsibility, they lead inevitably down the road to socialized medicine. Once government mandates the purchase of insurance, it must define what is to be included. The debate over the extent of coverage and soon over cost will become a political one, followed by increased government involvement in the marketplace. Medical savings accounts, in contrast, do not rely on government coercion. They place responsibility for health care decisionmaking squarely where it belongs—with the individual.

2. Lowering the Cost of Health Insurance

Medical savings accounts would allow people to substitute less costly self-insurance for more costly third-party insurance for small medical bills. To the degree they were self-insured, people would no longer face premium increases caused by the wasteful consumption decisions of others. And to the extent that third-party insurance was reserved for truly risky, catastrophic events, the cost per dollar of coverage would be much lower than it is today.

3. Lowering the Administrative Costs of Health Care

Because we rely on third parties to pay a large part of almost every medical bill, unnecessary and burdensome

---

[15] For example, the Heritage Foundation's proposal calls for requiring all individuals to purchase a minimum government-defined benefits package. See *A National Health Care Plan for America*, ed. Stuart Butler and Edmund Haislmaier (Washington: Heritage Foundation, 1989).

paperwork is created for doctors, hospital administrators, and insurers. By one estimate, as much as $33 billion a year in administrative costs could be saved by the general use of medical savings accounts.

4. Lowering the Cost of Health Care

Medical savings accounts would institute the only cost-control program that has ever worked—patients avoiding waste because they have a financial self-interest to do so. When people spent money from their medical savings accounts, they would be spending their own money, not someone else's—an excellent incentive to buy prudently. By one estimate, the general use of medical savings accounts would reduce total health care spending by almost one-fourth.

5. Removing Financial Barriers to the Purchase of Health Care

Under the current system, employers are responding to rising health insurance costs by increasing employee deductibles and copayments. Market prices are encouraging people who buy their own health insurance also to opt for high deductibles and copayments. One downside of this trend is that low-income single mothers and others who live from paycheck to paycheck may forgo medical care because they can't pay their share of the bill. Medical savings accounts would ensure that funds were available when a family needed them.

6. Removing Financial Barriers to the Purchase of Health Insurance during Periods of Unemployment

Under current law, people who leave an employer who had provided their health insurance are entitled to pay the premiums and extend their coverage for 18 months. Yet the unemployed are the people least likely to be able to afford those premiums. Medical savings accounts would solve that problem by providing funds that were separate from those available for ordinary living expenses. Medical savings account funds could also be used to purchase between-school-and-work policies or between-job policies of the types already marketed.

7. Restoring the Doctor-Patient Relationship

Medical savings accounts would give individuals direct control over their health care dollars, thereby freeing them from the arbitrary, bureaucratic constraints often imposed by third-party insurers. Physicians would see patients rather than third-party payers as the principal buyers of health care services and would be more likely to act as agents for their patients than for an institutional bureaucracy.

8. Giving Patients More Control over Insured Services

Every group health insurance plan includes some services and providers and excludes others. But the preferences of the group may not necessarily be those of the individual. In addition, state legislators are increasingly imposing their views on private group policies through mandated health insurance benefit laws. To the extent that individuals were self-insured, they could make such decisions for themselves.

9. Enjoying the Advantages of a Competitive Medical Marketplace

Patients who enter hospitals can neither obtain a price in advance nor understand the charges afterward. The evidence suggests that those problems have been created by our system of third-party payment and are not natural phenomena of the marketplace. When patients pay with their own money (as for cosmetic surgery in the United States and most routine surgery at private hospitals in Britain), they usually get a package price in advance and can engage in comparison shopping.

10. Enjoying the Advantages of Real Health Insurance

Because health insurance today is largely prepayment for

consumption of medical care, people with preexisting health problems often cannot buy insurance to cover other health risks. Medical savings accounts would encourage a market for genuine catastrophic health insurance and would make such insurance available to more people.

11. Creating Incentives for Better Lifestyle Choices

Because medical savings accounts would last people's entire lives, they would allow individuals to engage in lifetime planning and to act on the knowledge that health and medical expenses are related to their lifestyle choices. People would bear more of the costs of their bad decisions and reap more of the benefits of their good ones. Those who didn't smoke, ate and drank in moderation, refrained from drug use, and otherwise engaged in safe conduct would realize financial rewards for their behavior.

12. Expanding Health Insurance Options during Retirement

Medical savings accounts would eventually become an important source of funds with which to purchase health insurance or make direct payments for medical expenses not covered by Medicare during retirement. Such funds would help America solve the growing problem of long-term care for the elderly.

Using Medical Savings Accounts to Lower the Administrative Costs of Health Insurance

Health insurance not only creates perverse incentives, its overuse also leads to high and unnecessary administrative costs. For example, the cost of marketing and administering private health insurance averages between 11 and 12 percent of premiums.[16] A study by the American Medical Association has estimated that a physician spends six minutes on each

---

[16] According to estimates by Ray/Huggins Company, the "load factor" for private health insurance ranges from 5.5 percent for groups of 10,000 or more to 40 percent for groups of fewer than five people. See Uwe E. Reinhardt, "Breaking American Health Policy Gridlock," *Health Affairs* (Summer 1991), exhibit 1, p. 100.

claim and the physician's staff spends one hour on it and that physicians who contract with outside billing services pay about $8 per claim.[17] Medical savings accounts offer a way of cutting those costs dramatically while at the same time maintaining—and even improving—the quality of care.

Since patients would be responsible for paying most small medical bills, insurance companies would not have to process those small claims, which would, in turn, reduce the administrative cost of insurance policies. In many cases, processing a small claim can cost as much as the claim itself. Medical savings accounts would get the insurance company out of the business of processing small claims by having patients pay directly from their own medical savings accounts. Until patients reached their deductible, they would have little need to communicate with the insurer at all.

The reduced administrative costs would be passed back to doctors and hospitals, who would no longer be required to complete paperwork on behalf of insurers.

A Ballpark Estimate of the Economic Effects of Medical Savings Accounts

Various studies have compared administrative costs of health insurance in the United States with those of Canada's national health insurance program.[18] For example, Table 5.5 shows three estimates of the annual administrative savings

17 American Medical Association Center for Health Policy Research, "The Administrative Burden of Health Insurance on Physicians," *SMS Report* 3, no. 2 (1989).

18 For example, one study claimed that administrative costs in the United States were between 19.3 percent and 24.1 percent of total health care spending and accounted for more than half the difference in cost between the U.S. and Canadian systems. See Steffie Woolhandler and David Himmelstein, "The Deteriorating Administrative Efficiency of the U.S. Health Care System," *New England Journal of Medicine* 324, no. 18 (May 2, 1991): 1253-58. See also a critique of the study's methodology by the Health Insurance Association of America in *Medical Benefits* 8, no. 10 (May 30, 1991): 5. In another study, a national health insurance advocacy group, Citizen Fund, claimed that 33.5 cents of every dollar spent by private health insurance companies went for overhead expenses. See Richard Koenig, "Insurers' Overhead Dwarfs Medicare's," *Wall Street Journal*, November 15, 1990. The

Table 5.5

ESTIMATES OF THE ECONOMIC EFFECTS OF ADOPTING THE CANADIAN SYSTEM IN THE UNITED STATES

	Lewin/ICF	Physicians for a National Health Program	General Accounting Office
Savings in administrative costs			
Insurance overhead	-$22	-$27	-$34
Physician administrative expenses	-1	-9	-15
Hospital administrative expenses	-11	-31	-18
Total decrease in administrative costs	-$34	-$57	-$67
Expansion of coverage			
For the currently insured (based on RAND estimate)[1]	+$54	+$54	+$54
For the currently uninsured (based on RAND estimate)[1]	+19	+19	+19
Total increase resulting from coverage expansion	+73	+73	+73
Total net effect	+$39	+$16	+$6

SOURCE: General Accounting Office, *Canadian Health Insurance: Lessons for the United States*, June 1991, pp. 62-67; L. S. Lewin and J. Sheils, *National Health Spending under Alternative Universal Access Proposals* (Washington: Lewin/ICF, October 26, 1990); prepared for the AFL-CIO; and K. Grumbach et al., "Liberal Benefits, Conservative Spending: The Physicians for a National Health Program Proposal," *Journal of the American Medical Association* 265, no. 19 (May 15, 1991): 2549-54.

[1]Based on GAO estimates for increased hospital spending and GAO estimates increased to reflect the RAND Corporation results for physician spending.

that could be realized by adopting the Canadian system, as well as an estimate of the costs of eliminating out-of-pocket charges. The potential savings in administrative costs range from a Lewin/ICF estimate of $34 billion to a General Accounting Office (GAO) estimate of $67 billion.[19] However, the effect of eliminating all deductibles and copayments swamps those savings and leads to a net increase in costs.

We believe the estimates of potential savings from reduced administrative costs are much too high for three reasons. First, government accounting practices always lead to underestimates of the real cost of government provision of goods and services.[20] Second, the estimates completely ignore all indirect costs (for example, the costs of rationing and of physician and hospital responses to perverse incentives) caused by Canada's method of paying for health care. Third, many of the administrative activities in the U.S. health care system are not designed merely to control spending; they also are designed to prevent inappropriate medical care and maintain high quality. The United States is not likely to follow the Canadian practice of giving hospitals global budgets and forcing physicians to ration health care with few questions asked.

Nonetheless, Table 5.5 is interesting. What the GAO calculates as the rock-bottom cost of administering a health

results of other studies are reviewed below. For critiques of these estimates, see "GAO Report on Canadian Health Care Tainted by Charges of Partisanship," *Health Benefits Letter* 1, no. 16 (September 18, 1991); and the letters to the editor in *New England Journal of Medicine* 325, no. 18 (October 31, 1991): 1316-19. For a comprehensive comparison of administrative costs in the United States and Canada—one that concludes that there is very little difference between the two countries—see Patricia M. Danzon, "The Hidden Costs of Budget Constrained Insurance," Paper presented at an American Enterprise Institute conference, American Health Policy, Washington, October 3-4, 1991.

[19] See General Accounting Office, *Canadian Health Insurance: Lessons for the United States,* June 1991.

[20] See E. S. Savas, "How Much Do Government Services Really Cost?" *Urban Affairs Quarterly* (September 1979): 24.

Table 5.6

ECONOMIC EFFECTS OF COMBINING UNIVERSAL HEALTH INSURANCE WITH
MEDICAL SAVINGS ACCOUNTS AND HEALTH CARE DEBIT CARDS

Adjustment	Change in Costs ($ Billion)	
	Low Estimate	High Estimate
Savings in administrative costs[1]		
Insurance overhead	-$8	-$17
Physician administrative expenses	-5	-10
Hospital administrative expenses	-3	-6
Total	-16	-33
Coverage for the currently uninsured[2]	+12	+12
Behavioral response[3]	-90	-147
Total net effect	-$94	-$168

[1]Based on GAO estimates of the potential savings in administrative costs with the following adjustments: For high estimate, one-half of GAO savings attained in reduced insurance overhead, two-thirds of savings attained in reduced physician administrative costs, and one-third of savings attained in reduced hospital administrative costs; for low estimate, one-half of those amounts. See General Accounting Office, *Canadian Health Insurance: Lessons for the United States* (June 1991), Table 5.1, p. 63.

[2]Based on GAO and Lewin/ICF estimates. See J. Needleman et al., *The Health Care Financing System and the Uninsured* (Washington: Lewin/ICF, April 4, 1990), prepared for the Health Care Financing Administration.

[3]Based on RAND Corporation estimates. For high estimate, 23 percent reduction in total health care costs, excluding insurance overhead, research, and public health expenditures; for low estimate, spending is reduced by 45 percent for physicians and 10 percent for hospitals.

care system is probably high when compared with the cost of a system of medical savings accounts and health care debit cards. We have used the GAO method to estimate the potential reduction in administrative costs under a system of medical savings accounts and debit cards, and the RAND Corporation's method to estimate the likely reduction in health care spending if people had high-deductible health insurance. Table 5.6 shows the probable effects of a generalized system under which everyone (including Medicaid and

Medicare patients) has third-party catastrophic insurance and uses health care debit cards, drawing on individual medical savings accounts to pay small medical bills. As the table shows, a system that combines catastrophic third-party insurance with medical savings accounts should reduce administrative costs by as much as $33 billion. Because the presence of high deductibles would make patients more prudent purchasers of health care, total spending should go down by as much as $147 billion. After extending catastrophic health insurance to the currently uninsured, the net total savings is $168 billion, or almost one-fourth of what the United States now spends on health care.

Medical Savings Accounts and the Uninsured

Who are the uninsured? Basically, most uninsured Americans fall into one of four categories.

1. The Working Poor and Employees of Small Businesses

According to the Employee Benefit Research Institute, nearly 85 percent of Americans without health insurance either were employed or are dependents of employees. Agricultural workers were the most likely to be uninsured (nearly 42 percent had no health insurance). The four categories of nonagricultural workers most likely to lack health insurance were employed in nonprofessional services, retail trade, manufacturing, and construction. Nearly half of uninsured workers were employed by a company with 25 or fewer employees. According to studies by both the U.S. Small Business Administration and the National Federation of Independent Business, the number-one reason why such small businesses do not offer health insurance is cost. Part-time workers are far less likely to have insurance than full-time workers. That is likely due to the relatively higher cost of insurance per unit of productivity for employees who do not work full-time. Self-employed workers are also likely to lack health insurance.

2. The Young and Healthy

Surprisingly, studies have shown that a significant portion of the uninsured are not poor. Nearly 22 percent had incomes of more than $30,000, and 17 percent had incomes of more than $40,000. This group is composed largely of relatively young (nearly 60 percent are below age 30) and healthy individuals who have chosen to forgo the purchase of health insurance. They have generally decided—rightly or wrongly—that the benefits of insurance are not worth the cost.

3. The Temporarily Unemployed

Of those Americans without health insurance at any given time, half are uninsured for four months or less, and only 15 percent are uninsured for more than two years.[21] There is some overlap between this category and those working for small businesses, but a significant portion are individuals who are temporarily unemployed because they are between jobs.

4. The Medically Uninsurable

Much of the debate over health care is being driven by the undeniably difficult situation of a relatively small number of people—those with preexisting medical conditions, such as AIDS, cystic fibrosis, or diabetes, that make it difficult or impossible for them to purchase insurance. While the plight of those individuals should not be minimized, they represent only about 1 percent of the U.S. population. According to the U.S. Department of Health and Human Services, fewer than 900,000 people have been turned down for insurance because of their health.

Medical savings accounts could make a big difference in making health insurance more affordable and available for many of those people. For example, medical savings accounts would make it far easier for small businesses to

[21] Katherine Swartz and Timothy McBride, "Spells without Health Insurance: Distributions of Durations and Their Link to Point-in-Time Estimates of the Uninsured," *Inquiry* 27 (Fall 1990).

offer health insurance benefits. The cost of offering a cata-strophic policy, with, say, a $2,000 deductible, and giving the employee $2,000 for a medical savings account is often far less than that of providing traditional low-deductible insurance. Moreover, because medical savings accounts would encourage high-deductible insurance, they would allow people to escape the costly burdens of state-mandated health insurance benefits. By one estimate, one of four unin-sured people has been priced out of the market by the cost of mandated benefits.[22] But mandates have much less impact on the cost of a $2,000-deductible policy than they do on the price of $250-deductible policy.

Self-employed individuals would also benefit. Currently, the lack of health insurance is 10 times greater among the self-employed than among those who work for others.[23] Medical savings accounts would allow the self-employed to receive a substantial tax break for saving for their health care.

Medical savings accounts would also be completely portable. One of the most serious problems of our current health care system is that insurance is so closely linked with employment. That means that people who lose their jobs or change jobs are in danger of losing their insurance. With medical savings accounts, those individuals would continue to have funds available to pay their insurance premiums[24] or to purchase health care during such temporary interruptions.

Twenty Questions and Answers about Medical Savings Accounts

1. How Would Medical Savings Accounts Be Administered?

Medical savings accounts would be administered by

---

[22] John C. Goodman and Gerald L. Musgrave, *Freedom of Choice in Health Insurance*, NCPA Policy Report no. 134 (Dallas: National Center for Policy Analysis, November 1988).

[23] Of the self-employed, 28.6 percent are uninsured. *Federal Tax Policy and the Uninsured: How U.S. Tax Laws Deny 10 Million Americans Access to Health Insurance* (Washington: Health Care Solutions for America, January 1992).

[24] Under the provisions of the Consolidated Budget Reconciliation Act of 1986, employ-ees are entitled to continue coverage for up to 18 months after they leave an employer.

qualified financial institutions in much the same way individual retirement accounts (IRAs) are. Individuals could exercise choice over the investment of account balances, with the same restrictions on the types of instruments the accounts could own as now apply to IRAs.

2. How Would Funds from Medical Savings Accounts Be Spent?

The simplest method would be by debit card. Patients would use their debit cards to pay for medical services at the time they were rendered. At the end of each month, the account holders' statements would show recent expenses and account balances. No more paperwork would be needed than with any other credit card.

3. What Would Prevent Fraud and Abuse?

To receive medical savings account funds, a provider of medical services would have to be qualified under IRS rules. Qualifying should be a simple procedure, involving little more than the filing of a one-page form. But if IRS auditors discovered fraudulent behavior, the provider would lose the right to receive medical savings account funds and would be subject to criminal penalties.

4. What Types of Services Could Be Purchased with Medical Savings Account Funds?

Any type of expense considered a medical expense under current IRS rules would qualify. In general, the IRS has been fairly broad in its interpretation of what constitutes a medical expense. An unhealthy step in the wrong direction, however, was the IRS decision to disallow cosmetic surgery. There is no apparent reason why the removal of a disfiguring scar or a change in facial appearance that improves employability and self-esteem is any less important than an orthopedic operation that allows an individual to play a better game of tennis or polo.

5. What Tax Advantages Would Be Created for Medical Savings Account Deposits?

Medical savings account deposits would receive the same tax treatment as health insurance premiums. Thus, under employer-provided health insurance plans, medical savings account deposits would escape federal income taxes, FICA taxes, and state and local income taxes. If the opportunity to receive a tax deduction or a tax credit for the purchase of health insurance were extended to individuals, their deposits to medical savings accounts would receive the same tax treatment. Medical savings account balances would grow tax-free and would never be taxed if the funds were used to pay for medical care or to purchase long-term care or insurance to cover long-term care.

6. What about Low-Income Families Who Cannot Afford to Make Medical Savings Account Deposits?

If low-income families can afford to buy health insurance, they can afford to make deposits to medical savings accounts, since the primary purpose of the medical savings account option is to enable individuals to divide their normal health insurance costs into two parts: self-insurance and third-party insurance. Currently, no tax subsidy is available for people who purchase health insurance on their own. Health insurance would become more affordable for the currently uninsured if they could deduct some or all of the premiums from their taxable income. It would become even more affordable through a system of refundable tax credits, which would grant greater tax relief to low-income people.

7. How Could Individuals Build Up Funds in Their Medical Savings Accounts?

One way would be to choose a higher deductible insurance policy and deposit the premium savings in a medical savings account. For most people, a year or two of such deposits would exceed the amount of theirinsurance deductible. Young people and people in low-cost areas might be allowed to make even larger deposits. An alternative (which tends to be revenue neutral for the federal government) would be to permit people to reduce the amount of their annual, tax-deductible contributions to IRAs, 401(k) plans, and other pensions and deposit the difference in medical savings accounts.

8. What If Medical Expenses Not Covered by Health Insurance Exceeded the Balance in an Individual's Medical Savings Account?

One solution would be to establish a line of credit so that individuals could effectively borrow to pay medical expenses. Repayment would be made with future medical savings account deposits or other personal funds. Another solution would be to adopt Singapore's practice of permitting family members to share their medical savings account funds. This concern would vanish as medical savings account balances grew over time.

9. How Would Members of the Same Family Manage Their Medical Savings Accounts?

Because family members often are covered under the same health insurance policy, it seems desirable to permit couples to own joint medical savings accounts and parents to own family medical savings accounts. In those cases, more than one person could spend from a single account. But even if family members maintained separate accounts, that should not preclude the pooling of family resources to pay medical bills.

10. What about People Who Are Already Sick and Have Large Medical Obligations at the Time the Plan Is Started?

Such people might be harmed by a sudden increase in the health insurance deductible unless transitional arrangements were made. Most would benefit from a high deductible in the long run, but they might suffer financially at the outset. One solution would be for employers to extend credit to employees who were especially disadvantaged, with the loans to be repaid from future medical savings account contributions. Another solution would be for employers to bear part of the burden of those expenses (in the case of special hardship) during the transition period.

11. What about People Who Have a Catastrophic Illness with Large Annual Medical Bills Likely to Last Indefinitely?

Most of those people would be disadvantaged if they had an annual deductible. A better form of health insurance would have a per condition deductible, which would be paid only once for an extended illness.

12. Are There Circumstances under Which Individuals Could Withdraw Medical Savings Account Funds for Nonmedical Expenses before Retirement?

A reasonable policy would be to apply the same rules that now apply to tax-deferred savings plans (for example, IRAs and 401(k) plans). Thus, nonmedical withdrawals would be fully taxed and would face an additional 10 percent tax penalty.

13. How Do We Know People Would Not Forgo Needed Medical Care (Including Preventive Care) in Order to Conserve Their Medical Savings Account Funds?

We don't. The theory behind medical savings accounts is that people should have a store of personal funds with which to purchase medical care. And because the money they spent would be their own, they would have strong incentives to make prudent decisions. Undoubtedly, some of their decisions would be wrong. But many decisions made under the current system also are wrong. With medical savings accounts, people would at least have funds on hand with which to pay their share of medical bills. And since people would have an incentive to protect future account balances to cover future medical costs, some would certainly spend more on preventive health care. Because we cannot spend our entire GNP on health, health care has to be rationed in some way. The only alternative to national health insurance, with rationing decisions made by a health care bureaucracy, is self-rationing, with individuals making their own choices between money and medical services.

14. Given the Increasing Complexity of Medical Science, How Can Individuals Possibly Make Wise Decisions When Spending Their Medical Savings Account Funds?

One thing people can do is solicit advice from others who have superior knowledge. For example, most large employers and practically all insurance companies have cost-management programs in which teams of experts make judgments about whether, when, and where medical procedures will be performed. Those experienced professionals could play an important role in helping patients make decisions about complicated and expensive procedures. But the professionals' role would be as advice givers only. We should let the experts advise and the patient decide. Moreover, the fact that individuals would maintain medical savings accounts would not preclude their taking advantage of employer-negotiated price discounts from providers or managed care programs.

15. Given the Problems That Major Employers and Insurance Companies Have in Negotiating with Hospitals, How Could Individual Patients Possibly Do Better?

The reason large institutions have so much difficulty negotiating with hospitals is that the institution is not the patient. And the reason patients who spent their own money would wield effective power is the same reason consumers wield power in every market—they can take their money and go elsewhere. Physicians, hospitals, and other health care providers would have considerable incentive to win their business. Moreover, medical savings accounts would not preclude individuals from using employers as bargaining agents.

16. What Would Happen to Medical Savings Account Balances at Retirement?

People should be able to roll over their medical savings account funds into an IRA or some other pension fund. Thus, money not spent on medical care could be used, after taxes, to purchase other goods and services. Alternatively, medical savings account balances could be maintained to purchase postretirement health care or long-term care or insurance to cover long-term care.

17. What Would Prevent Wealthy Individuals from Misusing Medical Savings Accounts to Shelter Large Amounts of Tax-Deferred Income?

An individual's total tax-advantaged expense for health insurance plus medical savings account deposits could not exceed a reasonable amount. One definition of "reasonable" is an annual medical savings account deposit that would equal the deductible for a standard catastrophic health insurance policy.

18. What about People Who Join Health Maintenance Organizations?

They would have the same opportunities as those who join conventional, fee-for-service health insurance plans. Note that because many HMOs are now instituting deductibles, HMO members would have incentives to acquire medical savings accounts. Their HMO premiums plus their deposits to medical savings accounts could not exceed a reasonable amount, however.

19. Under Employer-Provided Plans, Would Employees Have a Choice of Deductibles?

Permitting employees to make individual choices makes sense. Over time, different people would have different accumulations in their medical savings accounts and, quite likely, different preferences about health insurance deductibles. Accordingly, employers would have an incen-

tive to provide a range of benefit plans to suit different
employee needs.

20. What Would Happen to Flexible Spending Accounts Now Available to Some Employees?

Medical savings accounts would replace FSAs under
employee benefits law. Currently, employees who make
deposits to FSAs must use the money or lose it, typically
within 12 months. Similar deposits made to medical savings
accounts would have no such restrictions.

6.
A Further Agenda for Change

The message coming to our shores from virtually every corner of the globe is, free markets work and socialism, collectivism, and bureaucracies do not. For the most part, Americans welcome that message. But in the area of health care, the message is falling on deaf ears.

It is worth repeating, therefore, why the message is true. In a market system, the pursuit of self-interest is usually consistent with social goals. When an individual pursues his own interest, his actions usually benefit others as well. Precisely the reverse is true in bureaucratic, nonmarket systems. The social goal may be clearly articulated, but each individual in the bureaucratic system finds it in his self-interest to take actions that defeat that goal.

The hallmark of bureaucratic thinking is the belief that individuals don't matter. All that matters is the social plan and the intelligence and ability of the people administering it. The hallmark of the economic way of thinking is the realization that neither the plan nor the people who administer it matter very much. What really matters is what is in the self-interest of the individuals who actively participate in the system. Therefore, we must find ways of changing the institutional environment in which health care is delivered, with the goal of making problem solving a matter of individual self-interest.

What follows in this chapter are proposals for a broader Patient Power agenda—beyond the immediate reforms of instituting tax fairness and allowing medical savings accounts. All these proposals have in common the goal of creating a medical

111

care system based on competition and personal choice.

Creating Freedom of Choice in Health Insurance

The number of Americans without health insurance now totals as many as 37 million people.[1] One reason so many lack health insurance is the existence of state regulations. State-mandated benefits, along with other state regulations, are increasing the cost of health insurance and pricing as many as one out of every four uninsured people out of the market.[2] A reasonable solution is to allow individuals to buy no-frills health insurance tailored to individual and family needs.

In recent years there has been an explosion of state laws requiring health insurance policies to cover specific diseases and specific health care services. Those laws are called mandated health insurance benefit laws. In 1970 there were only 48 such laws in the United States. Today there are more than 1,000, with legislation enacted by every state in the union.

Mandated benefits cover ailments ranging from AIDS to alcoholism and drug abuse and services ranging from acupuncture to in vitro fertilization. They cover everything from life-prolonging procedures to purely cosmetic devices: heart transplants in Georgia, liver transplants in Illinois, hairpieces in Minnesota, marriage counseling in California, pastoral counseling in Vermont, and deposits to sperm banks in Massachusetts. Those laws reflect the influence of special-interest groups that now represent virtually every disease, disability, and health care service.[3]

---

[1] The Employee Benefit Research Institute, however, has estimated the number at 34.4 million; see Jill D. Foley, *Uninsured in the United States: The Nonelderly Population without Health Insurance* (Washington: Employee Benefit Research Institute, April 1991). Other estimates place the number closer to 30 million. See the review of the literature in Michael A. Morrisey, "Health Care Reform: A Review of Five Generic Proposals," Paper presented at a policy forum, Winners and Losers in Reforming the U.S. Health Care System, sponsored by the Employee Benefit Research Institute Education and Research Fund, Washington, October 4, 1990.

[2] See John C. Goodman and Gerald L. Musgrave, *Freedom of Choice in Health Insurance,* NCPA Policy Report no. 134 (Dallas: National Center for Policy Analysis, November 1988).

[3] Ibid.

Currently, 45 states require health insurance coverage for the services of chiropractors, 4 states mandate coverage for acupuncture, and 2 states require coverage for naturopaths (who specialize in prescribing herbs). At least 13 states limit the ability of insurers to avoid covering people who have AIDS or a high risk of getting AIDS. Forty states mandate coverage for alcoholism, 27 states mandate coverage for drug addiction, and 29 states mandate coverage for mental illness. Seven states even mandate coverage for in vitro fertilization.[4]

Collectively, state mandates add considerably to the cost of health insurance, and they prevent people from buying no-frills insurance at a reasonable price. As Figure 6.1 shows, mandated

Figure 6.1
INCREASES IN INSURANCE PREMIUMS CAUSED BY SPECIFIC HEALTH INSURANCE BENEFITS

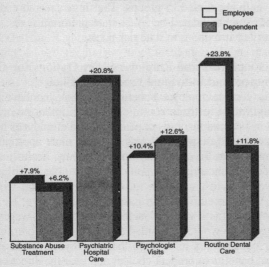

SOURCE: Gail A. Jensen (Wayne State University) and Michael A. Morrisey (University of Alabama at Birmingham), "The Premium Consequences of Group Health Insurance Provisions," September 1988, mimeograph.

[4] *Health Benefits Letter* 1, no. 15 (August 29, 1991).

coverage can increase premiums by 6 to 8 percent for substance abuse, by 10 to 13 percent for outpatient mental health care, and by as much as 21 percent for psychiatric hospital care for employee dependents.

Employees of the federal government, Medicare enrollees, and employees of self-insured companies are exempt from those costly regulations under federal law. Often, state governments exempt Medicaid patients and state employees. The full burden, therefore, falls on the employees of small businesses, the self-employed, and the unemployed—the groups that are increasingly uninsured.

Freedom of choice in health insurance means being able to buy a health insurance policy tailored to individual and family needs. That freedom is rapidly vanishing. To restore it, insurers should be permitted to sell federally qualified health insurance both to individuals and to groups. That insurance should be free from state-mandated benefits, state premium taxes, and mandatory contributions to state risk pools.

Giving Employers and Employees New Options for Cost Containment and Individual Freedom of Choice

Under current employee benefits law, employers have few opportunities to institute sound cost-containment practices without substantial income tax penalties, and employees have few opportunities to purchase less costly or more appropriate health insurance. To eliminate those problems, health insurance benefits should be personal and portable, with each employee free to choose an individual policy that would remain with the employee in case of a job change. Health insurance benefits should be included in the gross wages of employees who would be entitled to tax credits for premiums on their personal tax returns, so that employees would reap the direct benefits of prudent choices and bear the direct costs of wasteful ones.

Suppose a small firm considers purchasing an individual policy for each employee to take advantage of the favorable tax treatment of health insurance. As Table 6.1 shows, the firm is immediately faced with four problems. First, the cost of the policy varies with the employee's age (a 60-year-old male, for example, is about four times more expensive to insure than a 20-year-old male). The obvious solution is to pay the premiums for the policies and reduce each worker's salary by the premium amount. Second, not all employees want health insurance (for example, some may be covered by a spouse's policy). The obvious solution is to give health insurance only to those who want it, reducing the salary of each by the amount of the premium. Third, some employees may have preexisting illnesses for which the insurer wants exclusions and riders. The obvious solution is to negotiate the best possible deal for each employee. Fourth, employees may have different preferences about the content of their policies. Some may want to trade off a higher deductible for a lower premium. Others may want coverage for different types of illnesses and medical services (for example, infertility cover-

Table 6.1
SOLVING HEALTH INSURANCE PROBLEMS FOR
SMALL EMPLOYERS AND THEIR EMPLOYEES*

Problem	Solution
Costs differ by age, sex, type of job, and other employee characteristics.	Reduce each employee's gross salary by the amount of that employee's premium
Not all employees want or need employer-provided coverage	Give health insurance only to employees who want it
Some employees have preexisting illnesses	Negotiate the best coverage possible for each individual employee
Employees have different preferences about health insurance coverage (deductibles, services covered, etc.)	Allow each employee to choose a policy best suited to individual and family needs

*Each of these solutions requires changes in the tax law and employee benefits law to avoid costly tax penalties.

age). The obvious solution is to let each employee choose a policy suited to his or her needs and preferences.

Despite the obviousness of those solutions and the fact that each employee may gain from them, they are generally forbidden under federal law. In general, the tax law prevents employees from choosing between wages and health insurance and insists that all be offered the same coverage on the same terms. The result is that the employer must turn to a more expensive group policy with a package of benefits that no single employee may want. To make matters worse, the employer is forced to adopt a health care plan in which benefits are individualized but costs are collectivized.

Although large employers have a few more options, they, too, are forced into a system that has two devastating defects. First, because there is no direct relationship between health insurance premium costs and individual employee wages, employees see no relationship between the cost of employer-provided health insurance and personal take-home pay. Second, because there is no relationship between imprudent health care purchases and salary under conventional employer-provided health plans, employees have no personal incentives to be prudent buyers of health care.

In the face of constraints imposed by federal policy, employers are trying to hold down health care costs by taking actions that have very negative social consequences. Unable to adopt a sensible approach to employee health insurance, many large firms are asking employees to pay (with aftertax dollars) a larger share of the premium.[5] Often, employers pay most of the premium for each employee but ask the employees to pay a much larger share for their dependents.[6] Such

[5] In most large companies, employees can pay their share of the premium with pretax dollars under salary-reduction agreements with employers or through "flexible spending accounts." These options exist under section 125 of the Internal Revenue Code. However, the costs of setting up section 125 plans are often prohibitive for small employers. On the options for large employers, see Alain Enthoven, "Health Tax Policy Mismatch," *Health Affairs* (Winter 1985): 5-13.

[6] Kenneth H. Bacon, "Business and Labor Reach a Consensus on Need to Reduce Health Care Costs," *Wall Street Journal*, November 1, 1989.

practices result in some employees' opting not to buy into an employer's group health insurance plan. More frequently, they choose coverage for themselves but drop coverage for their dependents. Indeed, 3 million people who lack health insurance are dependents of employees who are themselves insured.[7]

Because employee benefits law prevents small firms from adopting a sensible approach to employee health insurance, many firms are responding to rising health insurance premiums by canceling their group policies altogether. Often, they then give bonuses or raises to their employees and encourage them to purchase individual health insurance policies (with aftertax dollars) on their own. Many employees, of course, do not do so. One of the great ironies of employee benefits law is that, although it was designed to encourage the purchase of health insurance, its more perverse provisions are increasing the number of people without health insurance. Because employers cannot individualize health insurance benefits, many are turning to other practices that are increasing the number of uninsured people.

To remedy those problems we recommend that (1) health insurance benefits be made personal and portable, (2) health insurance premiums be included in the gross wages of employees with tax credits for those premiums allowed on individual tax returns, (3) individual employees be given an opportunity to choose between lower wages and more health insurance coverage (or vice versa), and (4) individual employees be given freedom of choice among all health insurance policies sold in the marketplace.

If implemented, those recommendations would have five major advantages:

- Rising health care costs would no longer be a problem for employers, since health insurance premiums would be a direct substitute for wages.

---

[7] Employee Benefit Research Institute, "A Profile of the Nonelderly Population without Health Insurance," EBRI Issue Brief no. 66, May 1987, p. 7.

- Employees would have opportunities to choose lower cost policies and higher take-home pay.
- Employees would have the opportunity to select policies tailored to their individual and family needs.
- Employees would be able to retain the tax advantages of the current system but avoid the waste inherent in collectivized benefits.
- Employees would be able to continue coverage at actuarially fair prices if they quit work or switched jobs.

Introducing Freedom of Information in the Hospital Marketplace

Because they lack access to the necessary information, individual patients often are unable to play an effective role in containing hospital costs. In most American cities, patients cannot find out a hospital's total charge for a procedure prior to treatment. At the time of discharge, they learn there is not one price but hundreds of line-item prices for everything from a single Tylenol capsule to the hospital's admission kit. After a patient has been in the hospital for only a few days, a typical bill can stretch many feet in length. If restaurants priced their services the way hospitals do, at the end of an evening meal customers would be charged for each time they had used the salt shaker, taken a pat of butter, and had their water glasses refilled. There would, however, be this difference: at least they could read the restaurant's bill.

About 90 percent of the items listed on a hospital bill are unreadable. In only a handful of cases can patients both recognize what service was rendered and judge whether the charge is reasonable. For example, $15 for a Tylenol capsule is common but clearly outrageous, as is $25 for an admission kit. In other cases, patients may recognize the service but have no idea whether they are being overcharged. What's a "reasonable" price for an x-ray, a complete blood count, or a urinalysis? The patient who tries to find out is in for another surprise. Prices for items such as those can vary as much as five to one among hospitals within walking distance of each other, and in most cases the prices charged bear no relationship to the real cost of providing the service.

Patients who try to find out about prices prior to admission face another surprise. A single hospital can have as many as 12,000 different line-item prices. For example, for patients doing comparison shopping among the 50 hospitals in the Chicago area, there are as many as 600,000 prices to compare. To make matters worse, different hospitals frequently use different accounting systems. As a result, the definition of a service may differ from hospital to hospital.

Although hospital administrators do not have to give patients advance notice of their total bill, hospitals in Illinois are required to tell the state government. The following are some examples of total charges for outpatient services reported by Chicago hospitals in 1988: the charge for a mammogram varied from $13 to $127 (a difference of almost 10 to 1), the charge for a CAT scan varied from $59 to $635 (a difference of more than 10 to 1), tonsillectomy charges ranged from $125 to $3,365 (a difference of 27 to 1), and cataract removal charges varied from $125 to $4,279 (a difference of 34 to 1).[8] If patients knew about those differences, they could significantly reduce their medical bills. Unfortunately, most do not.

Hospital prices today are an unfortunate remnant of the system of cost-plus hospital finance. Because 90 percent of hospital revenue came from insurers who reimbursed on the basis of costs, a hospital's line-item prices were relevant only for a small fraction of the hospital's income—the 10 percent paid out-of-pocket by patients. Hospital line-item prices were used in some of the more complicated cost-plus reimbursement formulas, however. That gave hospitals an incentive to manipulate third-party reimbursements through

[8] Illinois Health Care Cost Containment Council, "A Report of Selected Prices at Illinois Hospitals: Outpatient Services," August 1989.

artificial pricing. Hospital prices quickly became artifacts rather than real prices determined by supply and demand.

We cannot possibly control spiraling health care costs unless patients can make prudent buying decisions. That cannot happen unless patients are given package prices prior to hospital admission. Accordingly, any hospital that receives Medicare money should be required to quote preadmission prices—either per procedure or per diem—to all patients. That is a requirement to quote prices, not an attempt to create price controls. Hospitals would remain free to charge any price to any patient.

What do hospital managers say about quoting preadmission, package prices for surgery? That depends. Publicly, they say that such a system would not work because physicians cannot predict in advance what complications will arise (and therefore what costs will be) with respect to any particular patient's surgery. Privately, they are already quoting package prices to major third-party buyers of health care. In late 1990, for example, the St. Louis Area Business Coalition on Health formally and publicly requested the area's 40 hospitals to voluntarily submit their retail prices for 205 different patient services. There was apparently considerable controversy about the proposal and what it might portend for the future. In a follow-up survey of the heads of state hospital associations, 73 percent of the respondents said they would oppose public disclosure of their retail prices.[9]

On the other hand, the practice of quoting preadmission prices is far more common than many people believe. In 1983 the federal government began paying fixed prices to hospitals for surgical procedures classified in one of 467 diagnosis-related groups (DRGs). Many states reimburse hospitals in a similar way through their Medicaid programs. Although hospital managers complain (justifiably, in many cases) that the DRG payments are too low, many hospitals

---

[9] David Burda, "Many State Hospital Association Presidents Would Resist Efforts to Establish Price Lists," *Modern Healthcare,* January 28, 1991, p. 34.

voluntarily charge (higher) DRG prices or fixed per diem prices to large third-party payers. In Nebraska, for example, Blue Cross reimburses almost all hospitals on the basis of prospective DRG rates.

A more radical move would be to combine the hospital charges with surgeons' fees and other charges in a single package price, covering all costs of surgery. A step in that direction was recently taken as part of a demonstration project undertaken by the Health Care Financing Administration, the organization that administers Medicare.[10] Medicare has contracted with four major hospitals to provide heart bypass surgery at fixed prices. When Medicare announced its intention to conduct its three-year project, more than 200 hospitals applied to participate. Although Medicare did not select hospitals on the basis of price, the agreed-upon prices are between 5 percent and 20 percent below the amount Medicare was paying when all of the components of the surgery were reimbursed separately.

The Medicare demonstration project is not unique. Individual hospitals and hospital groups are forming "centers of excellence" and bidding in a national market for the right to perform as many as 25 types of high-cost surgery. A Houston hospital, for example, has approached Blue Cross of Indiana with an offer to perform all of its bypass surgery for half of what Blue Cross would normally pay. With some of the best heart surgeons in the country, the Houston hospital offers high-quality surgery at a price that often includes the patient's airfare, as well as airfare and room and board (at the hospital) for the patient's spouse.

The concept of a package price covering all services has been common for years in cosmetic surgery. Similarly, some physicians or optometrists quote fixed prices for performing refractions and fitting contact lenses, and dentists often quote fixed prices for new dentures. Of course, the

10 Hilary Stout, "Medicare Starts Experimental Program to Curb Costs of Heart Bypass Surgery," *Wall Street Journal*, January 31, 1991.

underlying variation in costs for those procedures is small, so the provider is not at great risk when charging a package price. But in at least a third of the DRG categories, the variation in costs is also quite small. For high-ticket items such as heart surgery, costs can vary a great deal. But the market is showing us that, when the volume for these types of surgery is high, many hospitals are willing to charge a package price and accept the risk.

Encouraging Savings for Postretirement Medical Expenses

One of the greatest social challenges we face as we move toward the next century is paying retirement pensions and medical expenses for the elderly. Because both Social Security and Medicare are pay-as-you-go programs in which there is no current saving to meet future obligations, tomorrow's obligations will have to be met mainly by taxes on tomorrow's workers. The bill will be high. According to reasonable projections, by the year 2000, total health care expenses for the elderly will equal 14 percent of workers' payroll, and health care plus Social Security will equal 26 percent. By the year 2050, total health care spending for the elderly will equal 55 percent of payroll, and health care plus Social Security will equal 78 percent.[11]

Although the federal government subsidizes spending on current medical needs to the tune of $60 billion a year, individuals receive no tax subsidy when they save for postretirement medical needs.[12] Corporations also are greatly constrained by current tax law in their ability to set aside funds today for the postretirement health care expenses of their employees. As a result, the federal government is

[11] These projections are based on assumptions used in the Social Security Administration's pessimistic projections. See John C. Goodman and Gerald L. Musgrave, *Health Care after Retirement,* NCPA Policy Report no. 139 (Dallas: National Center for Policy Analysis, June 1989), Table III, p. 6.

[12] Jonathan C. Dopkeen, "Postretirement Health Benefits, Pew Memorial Trust Policy Synthesis 2," *Health Services Research* 21, no. 6 (February 1987): 810.

encouraging employers and employees to adopt the same pay-as-you-go approach that characterizes Medicare and other government health care programs for the elderly. Currently, unfunded liabilities for U.S. employers for postretirement health care exceed $300 billion. If those liabilities had been accounted for in 1989, they would have reduced corporate earnings of companies with postretirement health care liabilities by 33 percent—and their net worth by 30 percent.[13]

To address that problem, individuals and employers must be encouraged to save and invest today for future health care expenses. One method would be to use deposits to medical savings accounts, which would grow tax-free and provide funds for medical expenses (including nursing home care and insurance to cover long-term care) not now covered by Medicare. More is needed, however.

Individuals and their employers should be given tax incentives to contribute to medical savings accounts. Funds deposited to medical savings accounts would substitute for future claims against Medicare. By making annual contributions over time, people would rely more on private savings to support their postretirement medical needs and less on Medicare. Eventually, we would move to a postretirement health care system in which each generation paid its own way and in which postretirement health care dollars were the private property of the elderly, out of reach of politicians and special-interest bureaucracies.

Creating Catastrophic Health Insurance Coverage for the Elderly

The Medicare program pays too many small medical bills that the elderly could easily afford to pay out-of-pocket, but it leaves Medicare beneficiaries exposed to the risk of a catastrophic medical event, such as Alzheimer's disease,

---

[13] Mark J. Warshawsky, "Retiree Health Benefits: Promises Uncertain?" *American Enterprise,* July-August 1991, p. 63.

requiring an expensive nursing home stay. To address that problem, private insurers should be given the opportunity to repackage Medicare benefits and compete for customers on the basis of the package of benefits they offer.

A major reason why Congress was unable in 1989 to solve the problem of catastrophic coverage for the elderly was the fact that Medicare is a one-size-fits-all insurance policy designed for a very diverse group. Because the elderly who have few assets would be on Medicaid anyway, they are less interested in a catastrophic health care bill than in coverage for small medical bills. The elderly who have substantial assets are capable of paying several thousand dollars of small medical bills each year, but do need catastrophic coverage.

Private health insurers should have the opportunity to repackage Medicare benefits by offering private policies as an alternative to Medicare. The only required benefit would be catastrophic hospital insurance. If an elderly person chose a private insurer, the insurer would receive 95 percent of the actuarially fair value of Medicare insurance. For example, a private insurer might offer Medicare beneficiaries a policy with a $2,000 hospital deductible, a $2,000 physician deductible, and a combined deductible of $3,000. In return for those higher deductibles, the insurer might offer immediate nursing home coverage for Alzheimer's disease and an expanding nursing home benefit for other illnesses, depending on the number of years of coverage.

Currently, Medicare offers the 95 percent option to health maintenance organizations (HMOs), provided that they cover all of the benefits prescribed by Medicare. The same offer should be open to other insurers, who would compete for patients, and HMOs and other insurers should be free to repackage the benefits in ways attractive to Medicare beneficiaries. No one should be forced to participate, but alternative plans could provide needed services, equity, and efficiency for the beneficiaries.

Empowering Medicaid and Medicare Patients

Medicare and Medicaid are price-fixing schemes in which the level of reimbursement is often too low to ensure high-quality health care. The result increasingly is implicit and sometimes explicit health care rationing. To deal with that problem, Medicare and Medicaid patients should have the right to circumvent the normal reimbursement rules in ways that empower them and make them full participants in the medical marketplace.

In virtually every state, the people who matter least in the construction of health care programs for the poor are poor people. Far from empowering the indigent, the health care poverty industry consists of relationships between large bureaucracies in which poor patients are an excuse for the transfers of large sums of money.

The Medicaid program in many states pays about half as much as other insurers for comparable services. In itself, such a practice is not bad. Medicaid patients may have to wait for a hospital bed in order to obtain elective surgery, but in return for waiting they receive free medical care. What is bad is that they have no input into the terms of the discount or the conditions of the surgery, and they have increasingly fewer options in the market for any medical service. The reason is that Medicaid patients are not the principal clients of the medical community; the Medicaid bureaucracy is. The type of medical service the patients receive is often dictated by the amount the bureaucracy will pay. Patients cannot add to that amount to purchase higher quality service.

Nationwide, "good" doctors increasingly will not see Medicaid patients, especially for prenatal care. Some who do see them often practice revolving door medicine in which the objective is to service patients—and submit Medicaid reimbursement forms—as quickly as possible. To make matters worse, state laws generally prohibit nurse practitioners and physicians' assistants (including people who gave medical care to our troops in Vietnam and the Persian Gulf) from providing low-income patients with primary care services.

The result is a continuing deterioration in the quality of care that Medicaid patients receive. In some places, outright rationing schemes have been installed—schemes constructed by the health care bureaucracy, not by the patients themselves.

As an initial step toward empowering patients and dismantling the Medicaid bureaucracy, we should identify areas in which to suspend the normal reimbursement rules. Pregnant women on Medicaid, for example, should have an account to draw on for prenatal care. They should be able to add personal funds to that account, negotiate prices, and pay any amount they choose for prenatal care from any physician. They should also be allowed to share in any cost savings they achieve.

Similar reforms are needed under Medicare. Medicare's DRG system for reimbursing hospitals is not structured so that government is simply one more buyer in a competitive market. Instead, the system is a price-fixing scheme in which the government attempts to create an artificial market. Medicare literally fixes the price of services rendered, independent of supply and demand, forbidding hospitals to charge more than the DRG price even to patients willing to pay more. Medicare also prohibits hospitals from giving rebates to patients who use their services. Moreover, a single, national rate of reimbursement that ignores local differences is under consideration, and plans are also under way to include physicians' services in fixed DRG payments.[14]

Attempting to establish an artificial market creates perverse incentives for providers, which may adversely affect patients' health and may even increase health care costs. At the most basic level, in any price-fixing scheme the price can be set either too high or too low. If it's too high, the system encourages too many medical procedures, as was the case under pure cost-plus reimbursement. If it's too low, the system encourages too few.

In principle, the DRG price covers the average cost of treatment for hospitals that treat a wide variety of patients.

[14] See Robert Pear, "Government Seeks New Cost Control on Medicare Plan," *New York Times,* June 9, 1991; and *Modern Healthcare,* June 24, 1991, p. 48.

But it is unlikely that any particular hospital will have an "average" case load. Clearly, survival in the hospital marketplace under that system means attracting below-average-cost patients and avoiding above-average-cost patients. Who are the high-cost patients? They are the sickest patients, and more often than not they are low-income and nonwhite. For example, blacks and Hispanics have more severe illnesses, longer hospital stays, and (as Figure 6.2 shows) higher hospital costs than white patients, on the average.[15]

There is increasing evidence that hospitals are responding to the financial initiatives created by the DRG system. Thus, they give care readily and quickly to "profitable"

Figure 6.2
HOSPITAL COST PER ADMISSION BY RACE*

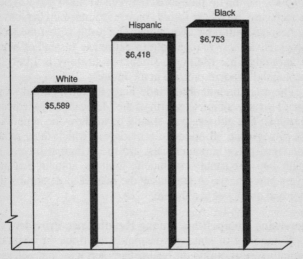

SOURCE: Eric Muñoz et al., "Race, DRGs, and the Consumption of Hospital Resources," *Health Affairs* (Spring 1989): 187.
*Based on admissions to Long Island Jewish Medical Center during 1985-87. Adjusted for DRG weight index.

[15] Eric Muñoz et al., "Race, DRGs, and the Consumption of Hospital Resources," *Health Affairs* (Spring 1989): 187.

Medicare patients, but slowly, reluctantly, and often of a lesser quality to "unprofitable" Medicare patients.

Another consequence of Medicare's method of payment is the rationing of medical technology. For example, although hearing loss is the most prevalent chronic disability among the elderly and affects almost one-third of all Medicare patients, Medicare's reimbursement rate for cochlear implants is so low that only a handful of Medicare patients have received the treatment.[16] Of about 68,000 Medicare beneficiaries who could benefit from the device, only 69 have received it under Medicare reimbursement—which makes each patient's odds of receiving the device only about 1 in 1,000. Currently, the cost of the operation plus the device is between $25,000 and $35,000. But on the average, Medicare reimburses only $10,500,[17] so the hospital loses between $14,500 and $24,500 on each case. Medicare forbids patients to make up the loss to the hospital with their own funds. The result is that the technology is virtually rationed out of existence. Instead of being an anomaly, that Medicare financing strategy is likely to become the standard practice in the future.

The recommendations made here are only partial steps toward a more complete reform of the Medicaid and Medicare programs. The ultimate goal should be to allow the beneficiaries to negotiate all prices in a market in which they, rather than third-party bureaucracies, are the principal buyers of health care. We should continue to limit the amount that taxpayers pay. But we should allow the market to determine the price and quality of health care.

Increasing Competition among Health Care Providers

A majority of state governments continue to maintain regulatory restrictions on health care services that act as a

[16] Nancy M. Kane and Paul D. Manoukian, "The Effect of the Medicare Prospective Payment System on the Adoption of New Technology," *New England Journal of Medicine* 321, no. 21 (November 16, 1989): 1380.

[17] "Proposed Rate for Prospective Payment of Cochlear Implantation," *Government Affairs Review* (September-October 1990): 7.

barrier to competition, such as certificate-of-need (CON) requirements. Those requirements say that if someone wants to build a new hospital, or buy a new piece of medical equipment, or offer a new type of medical service, he must first get permission from the government.

CON is based on the bizarre economic theory that greater supply and increased competition will lead to higher prices. However, studies have repeatedly demonstrated that CON programs not only fail to contain costs but may actually lead to increased costs, while limiting the availability of medical services, particularly in rural areas. The Federal Trade Commission has concluded that, on a national basis, "hospital costs would decline by $1.3 billion per year if states would deregulate their CON programs."[18]

Consequences of Change

If adopted, the proposals made in this chapter would not immediately solve America's health care problems. But they would empower individuals and create market institutions through which problems eventually would be solved by people pursuing their own self-interest. They would give individuals the incentive to solve problems that can never be solved through bureaucracies, regulations, or the power of government. The implementation of these proposals would constitute a national commitment to follow a path that is distinctly American in character—one that relies on individual choice and the efficiency of free markets.

[18] D. Sherman, "The Effect of Certificate-of-Need Laws on Hospital Costs: An Economic Policy Analysis," Federal Trade Commission, January 1988.

7.
Conclusion

The prevailing view is that markets cannot work in health care. That view has been used to justify the systematic suppression of prices and competition and their replacement by regulation, bureaucracy, and nonmarket institutions.

Yet a principal finding of this book is that individuals in the medical marketplace exhibit exactly the same self-interested behavior they exhibit in every other market. When consumers face artificially low prices for health care services, they overconsume those services. If the out-of-pocket cost is zero, they tend to consume health services until their value at the margin is zero. Self-interested behavior is also evident on the supply side. When suppliers of medical services find that overprovision of services is profitable, they overprovide. Moreover, they provide more of the services for which the rewards are high, and fewer of the services for which the rewards are low.

Virtually every major problem in health policy stems from those elemental facts. Whereas in normal markets the pursuit of self-interest usually leads to desirable social outcomes, in health care the opposite is true. The pursuit of self-interest in health care leads to socially bad outcomes precisely because all of the checks and balances found in other markets have been eradicated or undermined.

Every proposal to solve America's health care crisis with more bureaucracy and more regulation is based on the premise that self-interested behavior can be regulated and controlled, and perhaps eliminated altogether. For example, advocates of universal, free health care are not arguing for a system in which patients are allowed to consume any health service they happen to want without paying for it. The advocates fully realize that without constraints, free health care would bankrupt the nation. Rather, the advocates of national health insurance favor a system of health care rationing, under which patient preferences are largely ignored and medical services are delivered on the basis of technocratic judgments about medical needs. Similarly, the advocates of national health insurance are not arguing for a world in which physicians get paid for any services they happen to deliver. Rather, those advocates favor a system in which physician preferences are tightly controlled and the supply of health care services follows a national bureaucratic plan.

The assumptions of the advocates of greater government control are false. Self-interested behavior is a normal and natural characteristic of human beings that will always be with us. Socialism does not work in health care any better than it does in any other market. Wherever we find government allocating health care resources, we also find common, persistent patterns. The pressures produced by competition for political office inevitably lead politicians to limit expensive medical technology for the few who need it in favor of marginal services for the vast majority of people who are not seriously ill. Physicians and hospital administrators are invariably rewarded for achieving political goals, not medical goals. And the patients are the losers.

Health care systems ruled by politics are always inefficient. They do not deliver high-quality services promptly and efficiently because there is no market mechanism to reward the providers for doing so. The special victims of health care rationing in bureaucratic health care systems tend to be the poor, the elderly, racial minorities, and residents of rural areas. Moreover, all of the characteristics of government-run health care systems in other countries are increasingly evident in our own government programs—especially Medicaid and Medicare—which are answerable to self-interested bureaucrats and politicians.

In this book we have used the term "cost-plus finance" to describe the way in which Americans have paid for health care for the past 40 years. On the surface, that system appears very different from the national health insurance schemes of other countries. On a more fundamental level, however, our health care system shares with the systems of other developed countries one fundamental feature: the lack of a genuine marketplace. Whereas other countries have formally adopted socialism in health care, our preference has been for private-sector socialism. Yet it is increasingly evident that neither public-sector nor private-sector socialism in health care can provide Americans with what they want and need.

A unique feature of this book has been the elaboration of an alternative vision of how the health care system could function. We believe that it is senseless to try to eliminate self-interested behavior from the medical marketplace. To the contrary, self-interest must be channeled and encouraged—to solve social problems in health care the way problems are solved in other markets. That requires transferring money and power from large, bureaucratic institutions to individuals and encouraging vigorous competition in the market for health care services.

The difficulty is in getting from here to there. Before normal market forces can solve our most important problems in the health care sector, the cost-plus system must be dismantled from the bottom up. The most that politicians can do is to change the rules of the game. Once the rules have been changed, the tedious process of replacing cost-plus institutions with market-based institutions can begin. But the process of change must itself be market oriented—brought about by millions of people pursuing their own interests.

Market forces are already at work, chipping away at the cornerstones of cost-plus health care finance. Those forces are encountering formidable government barriers. The same public policies that enabled cost-plus health care to flourish are protecting it from collapse and replacement. The urgent need is for a reversal of policies, a removal of barriers to competition in health care. The change must be purposeful, coordinated, and designed to create a new health care system in which the preferences of individuals rather than those of impersonal bureaucracies govern the evolution of the medical marketplace.

The proposals set forth in this book have been designed to help the United States move to a market-based system. It is unrealistic, however, to expect major political change to occur on the basis of a vision alone. Political change always creates hardship. Therefore, in the very act of changing rules and regulations, politicians must be seen as solving immediate problems, as well as long-range ones.

It is for that reason that the policy proposals have two distinct goals. The first is to solve well-defined, immediate social problems in the health care sector, thus making the proposals politically attractive. The second is to create a public policy framework within which an ideal health care system can flourish and prosper.

If the recommendations in this book are adopted as national policies, virtually all the legal protections presently accorded to the system of cost-plus health care finance will have been removed. In response to those policy changes, market-based institutions will replace cost-plus institutions very quickly. What we have called an ideal health care system will rapidly emerge, and the market for health care will resemble other markets.

What will the new health care system look like? Although no one can be sure of the details, such a system is likely to solve the problems of ordinary people as well as major social problems in the health care sector. In the new medical marketplace, power will be transferred from huge bureaucracies to individuals acting on their own behalf. Patients rather than third-party payers will be the principal buyers of health care. Physicians will be the agents of patients. Hospitals will be businesses selling services to patients and physicians. Insurance companies will be insurance specialists only. Government will be simply a mechanism by which individuals become informed consumers in the medical marketplace.

No one can predict the changes that will take place in medicine in the 21st century. Fifty years ago, the most creative science fiction writers did not even come close to imagining what the practice of medicine would be like in the 1990s. Over the next 50 years, the changes almost certainly will be even more dramatic.

Of necessity this abridged volume has greatly simplified the complex medical, economic, political, and ethical issues surrounding health care reform. Readers interested in a more in-depth treatment of those issues should read the unabridged *Patient Power*, available from the Cato Institute.

Our generation has the opportunity to build a framework that will enable future generations to cope with the advances of medical science, whatever they may be. That is the legacy we can leave to our children, to our grandchildren, and to all others who follow.

About the Authors

John C. Goodman is president of the National Center for Policy Analysis in Dallas, Texas. Goodman earned his Ph.D. in economics at Columbia University and has engaged in teaching and research at six colleges and universities, including Columbia University, Stanford University, Dartmouth College, and Southern Methodist University. Goodman has written widely on health care, Social Security, privatization, the welfare state, and other public policy issues. He is the author of six books and numerous scholarly articles. His published works include *National Health Care in Great Britain, The Regulation of Medical Care: Is the Price Too High? The Economics of Public Policy,* and *Social Security in the United Kingdom.* In 1988 Goodman won the prestigious Duncan Black award for the best scholarly article on public choice economics.

Gerald L. Musgrave is president of Economics America, Inc., in Ann Arbor, Michigan. His Ph.D. is in economics from Michigan State University. He has engaged in teaching and research at California State University, Michigan State University, the U.S. Naval Postgraduate School, Stanford University, and the University of Michigan. Musgrave has written widely on health care and other issues. He is the author or coauthor of over 70 publications. He is the chairman of the Health Economics Roundtable of the National Association of Business Economists and is a Fellow of the NABE, the organization's highest honor. As a Reagan appointee to the National Institutes of Health, Recombinant DNA Advisory Committee, he approved the first human gene therapy protocols. He is the publisher of *The Right Guide,* the worldwide directory of conservative, libertarian, and traditional values organizations.

Please help support Patient Power!

- Buy copies of this book and give them to your doctor, your patients, your family, your members of Congress, your coworkers, your Christmas card list. Use the bind-in card or the coupon on the back page, or call **1-800-767-1241**.

- Get involved with one of these groups, which are working to implement the Patient Power plan:

> Americans for Free Choice in Medicine
> P. O. Box 1945
> Newport Beach, CA 92659-1945
> 714-645-2622
>
> Association of American Physicians and Surgeons
> 1601 North Tucson Boulevard #9
> Tucson, AZ 85716-3425
> 1-800-635-1196
>
> Cato Institute
> 1000 Massachusetts Ave., N.W.
> Washington, D.C. 20001
> 202-842-0200
>
> National Center for Policy Analysis
> 12655 North Central Expressway #720
> Dallas, TX 75243-1739
> 214-386-6272

Other books available from the Cato Institute

Patient Power: Solving America's Health Care Crisis
by John C. Goodman and Gerald L. Musgrave
The full story on how to rescue America's health care system from taxes, regulation, and bureaucracy. All the details on cost-plus health care, Medicare, Medicaid, health care in other countries, and how Medical Savings Accounts could give health care back to patients—in 673 pages, complete with 99 tables and 63 figures. 1992/673 pages/$16.95

What Has Government Done to Our Health Care?
by Terree P. Wasley
A concise and readable book showing how the problems in our current system stem directly from a long history of government meddling in the medical marletplace. Why the system is broken and how to fix it. 1992/162 pages/$10.95

Market Liberalism: A Paradigm for the 21st Century
edited by David Boaz and Edward H. Crane
Twenty-three essays on America's public policy problems, including taxes and spending, regulation, education, the environment, Social Security, health care, foreign policy, national defense, and poverty—and how the free-market, limited-government paradigm can solve them. 1993/352 pages/$15.95 paper

Sound and Fury: The Science and Politics of Global Warming
by Patrick J. Michaels
Virginia's state climatologist says that the popular vision of catastrophic global warming has no scientific foundation, charges Vice President Al Gore with "science by sound bite," and warns that we should not impose a $1-trillion cost on our economy on the basis of faulty science. 1992/196 pages/$11.95 paper

Liberating Schools: Education in the Inner City
edited by David Boaz
A dozen essays analyzing the problems in our schools and making a comprehensive case for educational choice—putting the power to choose in the hands of families. 1990/220 pages/$13.95 paper

Order these books toll-free 1-800-767-1241

YES! I support Patient Power, not government control of health care.

☐ Send me _____ copy(s) of this book.
   1 copy $4.95
   5 copies $15.00
   50 copies $100.00
   100 copies $125.00 $_____

☐ Send me _____ copy(s) of the full-length
   (673-page) *Patient Power* at $16.95. $_____

☐ I'd like to become a Cato Sponsor for
   $50 and receive regular reports on
   policy issues. $_____
                 TOTAL ENCLOSED $_____

Name _____

Address _____

City_____ State _____ Zip _____

☐ My check payable to *Cato Institute* is enclosed.

☐ Charge my ☐ VISA ☐ MasterCard

Account #_____ Exp. date_____

Signature _____

Send to Cato Institute, 1000 Massachusetts Ave., N.W.
Washington, D.C. 20001 or call toll-free 1-800-767-1241

YES! I support Patient Power, not government control of health care.

☐ Send me _____ copy(s) of this book.
    1 copy $4.95
    5 copies $15.00
    50 copies $100.00
    100 copies $125.00 $_____

☐ Send me _____ copy(s) of the full-length
(673-page) *Patient Power* at $16.95. $_____

☐ I'd like to become a Cato Sponsor for
$50 and receive regular reports on
policy issues. $_____
           TOTAL ENCLOSED $_____

Name _____

Address _____

City_____ State _____ Zip _____

☐ My check payable to *Cato Institute* is enclosed.

☐ Charge my   ☐ VISA   ☐ MasterCard

Account #_____ Exp. date_____

Signature _____

**Send to Cato Institute, 1000 Massachusetts Ave., N.W.
Washington, D.C. 20001 or call toll-free 1-800-767-1241**

YES! I support Patient Power, not government control of health care.

☐ Send me ____ copy(s) of this book.
      1 copy $4.95
      5 copies $15.00
      50 copies $100.00
      100 copies $125.00 $_____

☐ Send me ____ copy(s) of the full-length
    (673-page) *Patient Power* at $16.95. $_____

☐ I'd like to become a Cato Sponsor for
    $50 and receive regular reports on
    policy issues. $_____
              TOTAL ENCLOSED $_____

Name _____

Address _____

City_____ State _____ Zip _____

☐ My check payable to *Cato Institute* is enclosed.

☐ Charge my ☐ VISA ☐ MasterCard

Account #_____ Exp. date_____

Signature _____

Send to Cato Institute, 1000 Massachusetts Ave., N.W.
Washington, D.C. 20001 or call toll-free 1-800-767-1241